The Joy of Drinking

By the Same Author

In Private Life

Secrets of the Cat: Its Lore, Legends, and Lives

Hail to the Chiefs: Presidential Mischief, Morals, and Malarkey from George W. to George W.

One's Company: Reflections on Living Alone

Endangered Pleasures: In Defense of Naps, Bacon, Martinis, Profanity, and Other Indulgences

Bingo Night at the Fire Hall: Rediscovering Life in an American Village

Katharine Hepburn

Brief Heroes and Histories

Wasn't the Grass Greener?: Thirty-three Reasons Why Life Isn't as Good as It Used to Be

They Went Whistling: Women Wayfarers, Warriors, Runaways, and Renegades

Gentlemen's Blood: A History of Dueling from Swords at Dawn to Pistols at Dusk

When All the World Was Young: A Memoir

The Joy of
Drinking

Barbara Holland

BLOOMSBURY

Published by Bloomsbury USA, New York
Distributed to the trade by Holtzbrinck Publishers

All papers used by Bloomsbury USA are natural, recyclable
products made from wood grown in well-managed forests.
The manufacturing processes conform to the environmental
regulations of the country of origin.

Library of Congress Cataloging-in-Publication Data

Holland, Barbara.
The joy of drinking / Barbara Holland.
p.   cm.
ISBN-10 1-59691-337-1
ISBN-13 978-1-59691-337-0
1. Drinking of alcoholic beverages.   I. Title.

HV5020.H65   2007
394.1'3—dc22
2006039322

First U.S. Edition 2007

3 5 7 9 10 8 6 4

Typeset by Westchester Book Group
Printed in the United States of America
by Quebecor World Fairfield

Contents

Civilization Begins   1

The Jolly Tankard   22

Gin Lane   42

Pilgrims' Problems   55

Many Merrie Diversions   67

The March of the Drys   74

Martinis, Antifreeze, and Other Forbidden Fruit   81

The Following Day   100

"My Name Is David"   109

America Repents   117

Experts and Fashionistas   129

Appendix A—Making Your Own   141

Appendix B—Starting Your Still   145

Selected Bibliography   149

Civilization Begins

Quickly pass the social glass,
Hence with idle sorrow!
No delay—enjoy today,
Think not of tomorrow!

—Thomas Love Peacock

HERE ON MY SCRUFFY, untamed mountainside in northern Virginia, if you stand on the kitchen steps and pitch a rotten peach into the woods, in a few years you will have a fine peach tree. In years when May doesn't spring a sharp freeze and the squirrels don't, for reasons inscrutable, harvest the unripe crop, you will have more peaches than anyone can possibly eat or freeze.

It has always been so here. Long before, and during, and after Prohibition, my region was so famous for its peach brandy that the rich from all over the Northeast flocked here to stock up. Even the most industrious farmers learned early on that loading their carts with ripe peaches and trucking them to the market to sell at fluctuating unreliable prices while they bruised and rotted was no way to do business. Brandy was easy, portable, compact, and lasted pretty much forever. And among congenial company, more fun than eating peaches.

Farther north, the colonials drank their apples. It was easy. In an abandoned orchard, apples unpicked on the trees ferment themselves in the fall and possums climb up, get drunk, and fall down on their backs. Apples could be simply squeezed and the juice left around for a few days. Without modern preservatives, it turned into a two-fisted drink, but not a very respectable one; it was mostly for breakfast, not for dinner guests. Distilled, it turned into apple brandy, American cousin to Normandy's Calvados, the French workingman's eye-opener. Applejack was apple brandy distilled by freezing or simply mixed with straight alcohol.

The nostalgic notion of the family orchards is lovely— all that wholesome fresh fruit for our forebears to sit on the back steps biting into—but basically we were growing it to drink. So were people growing cashews, or sugarcane, or barley, or palms.

Some ten thousand years ago our ancestors gave up wandering around eating whatever came to hand and settled down to raise crops. Planting and harvesting was much more work than picking whatever they passed by, but incentives came with it. If you could stay in one place and cultivate fairly stable crops of peaches, rice, apples, berries, grapes, honey, potatoes, barley, wheat, milk, cactus, corn, sugarcane, coconuts, or practically any other organic substance, even if you didn't understand the science involved, it would presently ferment into a drink that made you forget your troubles and feel better about life.

William Faulkner, who knew a thing or two about it, observed that civilization begins with fermentation. For the record, fermentation is what happens when the glucose molecule is degraded to two molecules of the two-carbon alcohol known as ethanol, and to two molecules of carbon dioxide. It involved yeast, easily made by every husbandman and housewife from potato water and hops, or simply found naturally in various sources, as common as germs and everywhere, lurking on grapes, drifting into tubs of barley, settling on unpicked apples. Strictly speaking, yeasts are *Saccharomycetaceae,* or microscopic fungi. They feed on sugar, including the sugar in almost everything edible, and transform it into a drink with a punch.

The important thing was staying in one place instead of drifting, so things had time to ferment. The longer you waited, the more powerful the product, though some fruits, like mangoes, turned alcoholic almost as soon as they ripened, and even small birds passing by for a snack got too drunk to fly. And some fruits are just natural intoxicants; last year in South Carolina a flock of cedar waxwings came to grief after eating the holly berries in a downtown business park. The heady juice is irresistible and at least a hundred of them, flying drunk, crashed into a glass-paneled office building. Half of them died on impact.

In 2004 archaeologists dug up a batch of elegant, graceful jugs in the prehistoric village of Jiahu in China and found them to be between eight and nine thousand years old. Chemists inspected their contents: they'd been used for a wine made of rice, beeswax, and hawthorn fruits or wild grapes. Traces of similar brews had been found in the Middle East dating to around ten thousand years ago.

According to the evidence, their villages dated from the same time. Archaeological chemist Patrick McGovern observed, "The domestication of plants, construction of complex villages, and production of fermented drinks began at the same time in both regions."

Agriculture, drink, and social life walked in holding hands. We stopped living in mutually hostile family groups, scouring the brush for berries and beetles and throwing rocks at other families, and clustered together into tribes to grow and ferment crops. Having discovered conviviality, we moved our living quarters closer together and quit trying to kill each other on sight. Visited the neighbors. Shared a few drinks. Learned to work and play together. Had a few beers.

Beer has been called the cornerstone of civilization, though many claim honey's mead came first. Scholars speculate that a bowl of barley, first domesticated in the Near East, was left out and got wet, so the grain germinated and then was visited by airborne yeasts and foamed up, and somebody drank it and was pleased. That theory lays a lot of weight on a single bowl of Near Eastern barley. With no communication between peoples and areas, how did drinking spread so far so fast?

It seems almost like a supernatural inspiration, a blessing draped simultaneously over the peoples of the earth, and it seemed so to the ancients too, since before anyone understood yeast, natural fermentation was a glorious and often divine mystery. In Mexico the Aztecs drank pulque made from the agave plant, which graciously turned alcoholic just from being exposed to air. It was sacred. Getting drunk on it in a secular way was a capital crime, at least for the masses, while staying sober on it during religious ceremonies was equally illegal: The Aztec gods, particularly Tepoztecal, god of drunken merriment, had sent pulque as a miracle to the people and wanted to see it appreciated until everyone passed out cold.

In India today, followers of the thousand-year-old cannibal sect Aghori drink alcohol from a human skull in order to speak directly to the spirit and draw on its vast reserves of power and energy. Far away on the South Pacific island of Vanuatu, the natives drink enough of the fearsome kava, brewed from roots, to see and pray to a long-gone white man called John Frum, invisible to all but the blind drunk. In Japan the Shinto *o-miki* ritual requires the priest to drink so much sake that he can call up the sacred forces and ask them for good luck.

Unlike, say, iron smelting, gunpowder, or venereal disease, drinking didn't need to be carried from place to place by traders and travelers from more sophisticated cultures. It came naturally, everywhere.

When the Queen of Sheba visited King Solomon, according to Kings I, she was much impressed by the sheer numbers of his cupbearers, who apparently paraded past him in a steady stream while he emptied each vessel, and verily, "all King Solomon's drinking vessels were of gold." It's unlikely he'd have gone to such expense just to fill them with orange juice.

In the thirteenth century Marco Polo set out on his Asian travels and wandered the area from Arabia to Vietnam for twenty-four years, closely observing the native customs, products, food, and drink. Especially drink. Some Muslims, he tells us, drink copious amounts of wine and soothe their consciences by boiling it a bit first and calling it something other than wine, making it religiously acceptable.

In another area, though, Muslims drink their wine au naturel and lots of it. Polo finds it good but adds, "When it is drunk, however, by persons not accustomed to the beverage [perhaps himself?] it occasions an immediate flux; but upon their recovering from its first effects, it proves beneficial to them, and contributes to render them fat." On another trek near the Salt Hills of Thaikan, he finds an alarmingly bloodthirsty group of Muslims much given "to excess in drink, to which the excellence of their sweet wine encourages them."

According to the legend, the Prophet Mohammad was giving a dinner party for his followers from both Mecca and Medina, where everyone drank a sufficiency and one of the men from Mecca recited a rude poem about the tribe from Medina. A man of Medina, incensed, picked up a bone from the table and bashed the Meccan poet with it. The wound was slight but Mohammad was upset and asked Allah how to keep it from happening again. Allah answered, "Believers: Wine and games of chance, idols and divining arrows, are abominations devised by Satan. Avoid them, so that you may prosper. Satan seeks to stir up enmity and hatred among you by means of wine and gambling, and to keep you from the remembrance of Allah and from your prayers."

As with most rules, this was and is broken. Some authorities claim a good Muslim can drink all the wine he wants as long as he calls it medicine. The "Arabian Nights" puts it nicely: Wine, it says, "disperseth stone and gravel from the kidneys and strengtheneth the viscera and banisheth care, and moveth to generosity and preserveth health and digestion; it conserveth the body, expelleth disease from the joints, purifieth the frame of corrupt humors, engendereth cheerfulness, gladdeneth the heart of man and keepeth up the natural heat; it contracteth the bladder, enforceth the liver and removeth obstructions, reddeneth the cheeks, cleareth away maggots from the brain and deferreth gray hairs."

Hard to imagine a more sweeping commercial claim for any modern cure-all. The passage goes on, sadly, to say that "had not Allah (to whom be honour and glory!) forbidden it, there were not on the face of the earth aught fit to stand in its stead." It's easy to see where the author's heart lies, and he doesn't explain how, as a virtuous Muslim, he researched all those benefits.

I hear that today, in strict Islamic countries, drinks, being illegal, are so expensive that heavy drinking confers terrific social status, as during American Prohibition, proof of powerful connections and money to burn.

Several hundred years after Mohammed, coffee came to stand in for drink, and the gentlemen had an excuse to get away from the family by going to coffeehouses instead of taverns. However, there is little evidence that coffee is better than wine at quelling Islamic enmity and hatred as Allah promised.

Besides, alcohol is an Arabic word, *al-kuhul.*

Marco Polo continued on his travels. In Cathay he finds sake, "a sort of wine made from rice mixed with a variety of spices and drugs, so good and well-flavored that they do not wish for better. It is clear, bright, and pleasant to the taste, and being made very hot has the quality of inebriating sooner than any other." Polo did his homework.

In Samara he finds the palm wine "an excellent beverage," and so wholesome it's used to treat dropsy and complaints of the lungs and spleen. In Koulam he finds their local palm wine "extremely good, and inebriates faster than the wine from grapes." In Zanzibar he likes the rice wine too, and notes that the people give buckets of it to their elephants to inflame their courage before charging into battle, and in Muslim Aden he loves the liquor made from rice, sugar, and dates: "a delicious beverage."

There are various translations of Polo, and some have been cleaned up more than others. In R. E. Latham's version, on one of his northern journeys he finds a population much devoted to honey mead, and clubs of thirty to fifty men and women gather together to drink it all day.

> Let me tell you something that happened on one occasion. A man and his wife were going home in the evening after one of these bouts, when the wife paused to relieve herself. The cold was so fierce that the hairs of her thighs froze on to the grass, so that she could not move for the pain and cried aloud. Her husband, reeling drunk and distressed by her plight, stooped down and began to breathe over her, hoping to melt the ice by the warmth of his breath. But, while he breathed, the moisture of his breath congealed so the hairs of his beard froze together with his wife's and he too was stuck there, unable to move for pain. Before they could leave the spot, other helpers had to come and break the ice.

(I don't think we're supposed to believe that this hardy northern wife had luxuriant long hairs on her thighs; surely he's speaking delicately of another area. It's also possible that someone was pulling Polo's leg. He believed many a strange and marvelous report.)

All over the world drinking arose spontaneously and joyfully, complete with merry ceremonies. Even today all around the arctic circle, where temperatures drop to 96 below, among the Eveny nomadic reindeer herders, whose traditions go back maybe eleven thousand years, the guest entering the tent must still placate the Fire God by splashing some vodka on the burning logs. In many primitive cultures the elders must drink themselves into a stupor, then wake to reveal the intentions of the gods and the plans of the enemies.

In Central Asia the nomadic Mongolians never stood still long enough to raise a crop. Their only available raw material was horses and lots of them, so in the absence of grapes, barley, or honey, they fermented mares' milk into *airag*. According to the online magazine *Mongolia Today,* it gets up only to 18 proof or so, so the trick is to drink lots of it: "Drinking too much airag, one may easily become drunken, especially given the fact that usually airag is served in huge bowls. Medical features of airag were proven long time ago. It clears any poison, especially the consequences of much fat consumed during long winter, strengthens the body. It contains many types of vitamins, organic and mineral elements. Airag is widely used for treatment of many diseases."

The magazine claims it's prepared in great vats and must be stirred, with family and visitors helping, a thousand times a day. Apparently, though, if you were on the move, the technique was to sew it up tightly into a horsehide and keep beating it, or just tie it to a trotting horse all day.

Marco Polo said it was fermented "in such a manner that it has the quality and flavor of white wine," but a more recent traveler reports that it tastes like vomit. Another said it reminded him of warm sake filtered through a dirty horsehair sock.

In the eighteenth century when Captain Cook arrived in Tahiti, the easy-going natives had been living happily on a small island thousands of ocean miles from anyone since time out of mind. They knew nothing about civilization except singing and dancing, and almost the only work they did was brewing up a native drink they called *ava*. They drank it out of coconut shells and were very merry.

In the nineteenth century the British explorer Capt. Sir Richard Burton plunged into Central Africa from the east coast and forged into uncharted areas where the people were so primitive he hesitated to call them "people." Nobody had ever stopped by to teach them, but they'd figured it out for themselves and drank a wine they called *pombe,* made from plantains, and it gave every satisfaction. According to Burton, they started drinking as soon as they got up in the morning and stayed pretty much drunk till they fell asleep again. Their revered tribal queen mother was almost never sober; he saw her get down on her knees and suck up the *pombe* from a trough. (Burton, a Victorian gentleman, was fairly disgusted, though his own ancestors probably had a beer or two.)

In the twentieth century the intrepid Irish traveler Dervla Murphy wandered off the beaten paths on foot, bicycle, or mule. Unlike most gentleman travelers in such places, who needed twenty to forty native bearers with camels, llamas, or mules to carry their supplies of brandy, canned meat, tins of salmon, Fortnum & Mason's marmalade, and other heavy essentials, Murphy is a minimalist. She eats and drinks whatever she comes across, drawing the line only at Coke and Pepsi. She believes that rum and lots of it will cure whatever ails her; she cheerfully swigs beer from a bottle being passed around by an obviously tubercular gathering. In Pakistan she drinks a wine-like concoction fermented in a lightly cured sheepskin, which not surprisingly tastes like dead sheep.

In Coorg the Sikkimese ragi beer packs such a surprising wallop that she keels over in mid-journal-entry, but adds that the local strong drink made of cashew nuts is much deadlier. Whatever problems the night bequeaths her, she refreshes herself in the morning, breakfasting on a liter of palm-toddy beer, delicious even when the neck of the bottle is thick with ants. Sometimes nobody even has a name for what she's drinking and she can judge it only by its alarming effects: in Nepal the local raki struck her stone-blind for twenty-four hours. In Madagascar she finds a marvelous local tipple which she enjoys inordinately until she finds out it's made from the sap of the Man-Eating Tree and killed many a French colonial. It gives her gout, but she forges on.

In 1988, deep, deep in the Amazonian jungle where perhaps no stranger's foot had trod before, Redmond O'Hanlon, in *In Trouble Again,* sampled the local *aguardimente,* a firewater cooked up from molasses, anise, and assorted local extras. The next day he found the aftereffects easily controlled, once the vomiting stopped, with heavy doses of Imodium; he had no genetic defenses. The natives revere it and consider it the national drink and symbol, the very heart and soul of Colombian culture and identity, as a grape version of it is revered in Peru and Chile.

In the twenty-first century a Nigerian wrote to *Harper's* of the joys of *burukutu*, a native beer made from sorghum: "This drink is pure and natural. That is why after taking even a whole pot of it, one never suffers from a hangover the next morning; rather, one is stronger and more active . . . I love this African beer because the spirit of African communion comes alive wherever it is present."

Drink, the social glue of the human race. Probably in the beginning we could explain ourselves to our close family members with grunts, muttered syllables, gestures, slaps, and punches. Then when the neighbors started dropping in to help harvest, stomp, stir, and drink the bounty of the land, after we'd softened our natural suspicious hostility with a few stiff ones, we had to think up some more nuanced communication, like words. From there it was a short step to grammar, civil law, religion, history, and "The Whiffenpoof Song."

It's almost impossible to believe now, with limitless professional amusement at our fingertips, but for many thousands of years the only entertainment people had was other people. Now we can avoid our fellow humans completely for weeks, companioned only by electronics, and have a fine time, but for millennia we had to put up with people and their jokes, their long boring stories, their boasts and card tricks and primitive musical instruments, or spend the evening staring at the wall.

Alcohol helped. After a couple of drinks, even our hairiest neighbors had their charms, and our own wit rang in our ears like Noel Coward. Along with occasionally promoting drunken brawls, alcohol encouraged a more tolerant interest in one's fellow man. Note that today vodka-soaked Russia doesn't produce murderous fanatics like those of caffeine-soaked Islamic societies. Drunk, the suicidal Russian kills only himself.

We like to think we live now in an age of unprecedented stress, full of cell phones, nuclear threats, looming epidemics, and terror alerts, but life back then may have had stresses of its own, like tigers and freezing to death, and a swallow of fermented juice may have cheered up our ancestors even more than it cheers ourselves. These ancestors spent much of their lives in pain from abscessed teeth, festering wounds, spider bites, and broken bones, and in fear of thunder, lightning, ghosts, witches, and wolves. Anything that blunted the ache and soothed the terror must have seemed like a gift from the mysterious gods.

Religions sprang up around drinking. In *The Golden Bough,* Sir James Frazer tells us, disapprovingly, "The god Dionysus or Bacchus is best known to us as a personification of the vine and of the exhilaration produced by the juice of the grape. His ecstatic worship, characterized by wild dances, thrilling music, and tipsy excess, appears to have originated among the rude tribes of Thrace, who were notoriously addicted to drunkenness . . . The religion spread like wildfire through Greece until the god whom Homer hardly deigned to notice had become the most popular figure of the pantheon." And a fine time was had by all.

There's a story that the invincible Alexander the Great died after almost winning a drinking contest.

We learned in school that the Romans conquered the world because of their superior discipline and stern self-control, but this must have been confined to the actual battlefield and didn't constrain private life. It seems it's not true that their banquet halls had a separate antechamber in which to throw up; apparently they were much more casual about the matter: vomit was simply a by-product of the good life. The noble Marc Antony, lover of Queen Cleopatra, he who speaks so eloquently at Caesar's funeral in Shakespeare, was dearly beloved by his soldiers because of his fine roisterings with them. Even Cleopatra was mildly revolted by his habits, and on at least one documented occasion, after an all-night party, he had a public address to deliver, stood before the assembled populace, and threw up in his sandals while a friend held his robe to one side to keep it from getting splattered.

The joys of drink were by no means confined to the rough-hewn military. In Marc Antony's day, the last century B.C., the Roman poet Horace burst into praise:

Think of the wonders uncorked by wine! It opens secrets,
gives heart to our hopes, pushes the cowardly into battle,
lifts the load from anxious minds, and evokes talents.
Thanks to the bottle's prompting no one is lost for words,
no one who's cramped by poverty fails to find release.

Alas, the upper-caste Romans were drinking their wine out of lead goblets, and over time the alcohol dissolved the lead, which got swallowed, and the upper-caste ladies went sterile, and the upper-caste gentlemen went a bit unreliable in the head, the barbarians stormed the gates, and Rome fell. In the meantime, though, it was quite a party.

Jesus, taking pity on the guests, changed the water into wine. The Catholic Church decreed that wine—real wine, not grape juice—is transformed into the actual blood of Christ at the ceremony of the Eucharist, though the celebrants aren't supposed to run wild and dancing. At the Jewish Passover seder, everyone at the table, including children, is required to drink a minimum of four cups of wine, each cup to hold a minimum of three and a half ounces.

Early on, nobody cared what it tasted like. Only the kick counted. And though they may not have noticed, in northern climates fermentation improved the general health, with fruits and cereals drinkable all winter long. Beer's sprouted barley had enzymes that convert starches to sugars, making them more digestible, and its yeast held amino acids and increased the B vitamins. The *American Journal of Clinical Nutrition* claims that a moderate beer drinker—whatever that means—swallows 11 percent of his dietary protein needs, 12 percent of the carbohydrates, 9 percent of essential phosphorus, 7 percent of his riboflavin, and 5 percent of niacin.

Should he go on to immoderate beer drinking, he becomes a walking vitamin pill.

Almost everyone found something interesting to drink and held it dear and often holy. The rest found native plants to chew or burn and inhale, spiriting away their troubles. South American coca leaves, thoughtfully sucked, are cheering and strengthening, though eventually your teeth turn black. Deep in the Venezuelan jungle, something called *yappo* is popular among the fiercer tribes. It's made of assorted bark and leaves, which they blow into each other's noses. The resulting pain to ear, nose, and throat is said to be horrendous, but well worth it for the grand hallucinations. Betel is native to India, Malaya, and Java, where even the youngest children find the leaves pleasantly stimulating. Perfectly legal, perhaps because the authorities don't know what it is, it's currently for sale all over the Internet.

It's said that when the Europeans found them, the American Indian tribes were happy with tobacco in the east and assorted natural hallucinogens elsewhere, and knew not drink. Apparently this isn't strictly true; like everyone else they'd stumbled on fermentation, and they drank enough to induce mystical trances and communicate with the gods. The white man's offerings were something else again. Rum and gin aren't blackberry wine. The Spaniards fetched strong drink to Mexico and South America in the 1500s and Henry Hudson sailed into New York in 1609 with many casks. The natives were immediately captivated, but it wasn't very good for them. Eager to spread the joys of civilization, the newcomers passed out the firewater and made quite a profit on it, too. Russian fur traders in Alaska cut many a slick deal with the Eskimos, trading whiskey for skins. Our own noble pioneer ancestors facilitated their pacts and land-grabs and fur trades with dollops of booze for the natives; it's said that every Indian treaty was soaked in alcohol.

With no ancestral acquaintance with the stuff, maybe even with some quirk in their genetic makeup, it brought them more sorrow than joy.

Civilization brought specialization and leisure. People released from plowing and killing tigers all day had time for the arts and sciences, like improving what they drank. The ancient Sumerians, in what we were told in school was the cradle of all civilization, made eight different kinds of barley beer, eight of wheat beer, and several of a blend. They worshipped a special goddess in charge of nothing but beer.

By 2000 B.C. the Egyptians were combining baking and brewing. They steeped the barley in water until it made a paste, then set it out to dry and season for a while, and baked it—slightly—into bread, which they soaked in water. This they left in a warm place till it fermented, then they squeezed out its delicious juices into a pot and drank them. I suppose after the bread had served its purpose they fed it to the pigs, since people ate bread only in times of famine, and the pigs rejoiced.

The beer juice, delicately flavored with rue, coriander, juniper, dates, tarragon, anise, or licorice, was so good that many guests threw up. A fresco from the second millennium B.C. shows an Egyptian lady of quality at a banquet turning delicately from the table to throw up into a bowl held out by a servant for the purpose.

Hammurabi, ruler of Babylon from 1795 to 1750 B.C., gave the world its first written code of laws, and regulating beer figured prominently among them. Any tavern keeper presumed to be cheating on the quantity of beer she gave out in exchange for corn should be convicted and thrown into the water to drown.

By 1500 B.C. the elegant niceties of germinating assorted cereals were established as an art form; Egyptians sent their dear departed into the next world with one for the road; taverns flourished. An Egyptian abstinence warning from 1400 B.C. says to be careful about getting drunk in taverns, because your companions may "repeat words which may have gone out of your mouth, without your being aware of having uttered them."

In India they were making a sophisticated wine out of rice, grain, sugar, molasses, and honey. They drank it and gave some to their mistresses, but their wives were allowed only to sniff, not drink it. It smelled lovely.

The Chinese paid homage to their gods by drinking wine while sacrificing some of their countrymen, puddling the ground with a mix of blood and fermented grape juice.

Fermenting refinements distracted nobody from the basic purpose of drinking, as our connoisseurly refinement has distracted us in current times. When Noah, the favored of the Lord, got out of the ark, the first thing he did as a husbandman was plant a vineyard and get roaring drunk on its fruits. He savored neither its nose nor its finish, neither did he compare it to woodsmoke or apples, and he lived on for another 350 years, happy as a clam.

Drink that cheered the human condition was a basic purpose of agriculture, not just a by-product. Aristotle considered grapes inedible, being merely a larval phase of wine. Drink was a wholesome necessity in the diet, friend of body as well as soul, and toasts were raised "to your health!" and "à votre santé!" Socrates said wine "does of a truth moisten the soul and lull our griefs to sleep." Moisten the soul: a cheerful thought.

Though sociable in most times and places, drink was also essential to galvanize the warrior when warfare was called for; disarming the natural sense of caution, it led him whooping into battle. Unfortunately the exact quantity needed was hard to calculate and sometimes problems arose. Rumor has it that the Saxons lost England in 1066 because their army was a bit too drunk at the Battle of Hastings and the Normans were sober, or at least less drunk, though after they'd occupied the place they learned to drink like Saxons. And certainly when George Washington swooped down on the Hessian troops in Trenton, there was scarcely a sober Hessian. The Hessians, like the drunk Danes in Beowulf's mead-hall when Grendel swooped down on them, never knew what hit them.

Up until the day before yesterday, as history goes, making what we drank was an ordinary household chore, like cooking dinner. The housewife either did it herself or supervised the servants. She was in charge. Perhaps our ancestors still had one too many on occasion, but it's unlikely they spent the evening beating their wives, who might have popped them on the head with a spoon and locked up their supplies.

Beer, mead, or ale, wholesome and nourishing, was the staple drink of the virtuous. Queen Elizabeth was extremely fond of good English ale, putting away royal quantities of it, and spoke out firmly against importing frivolous foreign wine.

In *The Diary of a Country Parson, 1758–1802,* Parson Woodforde is a bachelor and, though he buys his rum, gin, and cognac from a smuggler, he makes his own mead and beer, both "strong beer" and "table beer," the latter perhaps for children. He tells us, "Busy most part of the Afternoon in making some Mead Wine, to fourteen Pound of Honey, I put four Gallons of Water, boiled it more than an hour with Ginger and two handfuls of dried Elder-Flowers in it, and skimmed it well. Then put it into a small Tub to cool, and when almost cold I put in a large gravey-Spoon full of fresh Yeast, keeping it in a warm place, the Kitchen during the night."

In Germany beer soup was the standard family breakfast, the toast-and-coffee of its day, till the end of the eighteenth century. In *Tastes of Paradise,* Wolfgang Schivelbusch gives us a recipe, though he says there were simpler versions:

> Heat the beer in a saucepan; in a separate small pot beat a couple of eggs. Add a chunk of butter to the hot beer. Stir in some cold beer to cool it, then pour over the eggs. Add a bit of salt, and finally mix all the ingredients together, whisking it well to keep it from curdling. Finally, cut up a roll, white bread, or other good bread, and pour the soup over it. You may also sweeten to taste with sugar.

In family portraits of the day, the results are clear: everyone looks extremely well-nourished and even the youngest children have extra chins.

Home drinking was decorous. Public taverns weren't, and competitive drinking bouts were popular, especially in Germany and Scandinavia. Everyone had to drink a toast to everyone else, and then everyone responded until nobody was left standing; to try to quit while you could still walk was an insult to all. A fifth-century Roman, traveling through Germany, describes one particularly gruesome drinking competition, and a thousand years later another writer says, according to Schivelbusch, "These guests and drunkards contend with each other, man to man, in pairs:

they must swallow half, then all of a drink in one gulp, and without stopping to take a single breath, or wiping their beards, until they sink into a complete stupor." Woodcuts and lithographs of the taverns of the time usually included at least one man throwing up on the floor.

As Mark Twain sagely observed, "Sometimes too much drink is barely enough."

The Jolly Tankard

See, the welcome Brewhouse rise,
See, the priest his duty plies!
And with apron duly bound,
Stirs the liquor round and round.
O'er the bubbling cauldron play
Mirth and merriment so gay;
Melancholy hides her head—
The frowns of Envy all are fled;
Youthful wit and attic salt
Infuse their savour in the Malt.

—OLD DRINKING SONG

THE TAVERN, BAR, PUB, local, cafe, *shebeen,* or what-have-
you has always been the evening refuge, escape from the
dark and dangers of the night, witches and ghosts, family
and work. In the countryside, escape from silence and
loneliness, along with a chance to hear some news of the
wider world; a spot of gossip, crop prices, and the rise and
fall of empires. In cities, the place to meet neighbors you
would never otherwise meet and weave together a social
family out of the loose strings of strangers. Everywhere, the

nourishing contact with humans, known and new. What E. B. White called "the golden companionship of the tavern."

In the modern coffeehouse your fellow customers, edgy with caffeine, are hyperactive, suspicious by nature, busy with laptops. Avoiding eye contact. In the tavern, to belly up to the bar with an iPod in your ear or whip out a cell phone and talk to persons not present is considered mildly bad form, but it's good manners in the coffeehouse, signaling that you won't be bothering anyone else, eavesdropping, or trying to strike up an acquaintance.

Historically, in a proper pub everyone there is potentially, if not a lifelong friend, at least someone to lure into an argument about foreign policy or the Red Sox. Camaraderie is expected. Alcohol builds a bridge between strangers, or so it was for thousands of years until the recent arrival of television, after which people could sit elbow to elbow, night after night, gazing only at the stock car races, and even the once-attentive bartender gazes at the screen, towel dangling from his hand, and treats requests for beer as interruptions.

To extract the fullest flavor of our drinking house, we needed to spend serious evening time there, slowly coming to know the bartender and the regulars, their joys and sorrows. Getting promptly snockered on strong spirits defeated the purpose. Taverns were the natural home of long, slow draughts of beer. Or in sunnier countries, long, slow bottles of wine.

In early times, the problem with beer was that it didn't wait around long. Archaeologists have recently discovered in the Peruvian Andes a thousand-year-old brewery with twenty brewing vats, probably a state-sponsored institution. The beer, called *chicha,* was brewed from the berries of the pepper tree, and it spoiled within a week. The brewery turned out several hundred gallons at a time. This meant that all the citizens for miles around had to drop everything, race over, and gather round and gulp it down manfully on the spot. This must have made for a hell of a party.

Time passed. Preservation improved. We could slow down over our pints. Linger at the tavern.

You went to the pub more for the company than the beer, since beer was the staff of life at home. It was, like Parson Woodforde's, brewed at home and drunk there for breakfast, lunch, and dinner, and it was served out freely on many jobs, as a perk. In his splendid 1969 book, *Akenfield: Portrait of an English Village,* Ronald Blythe talked to an old farmer whose memories went back into the nineteenth century. He remembers when fields were harvested by hand, with scythes, and beer was part of the bargain. Each man was allotted and expected to drink seventeen pints, or about two gallons, a day. Field work: you sweat off a lot.

> You boiled five or six pails of water in a copper. Then you took one pail of the boiling water and one pail of cold water and added them together in a tub big enough to hold eighteen gallons. You then added a bushel of malt to the water in the tub. You then added boiling water from the copper until there was eighteen gallons in the tub. Cover up and keep warm and leave standing for at least seven hours, although the longer the better. When it has

stood, fill the copper three parts full from the tub, boil for an hour and add half a pound of hops. Then empty into a second tub. Repeat with the rest. All the beer should now be in one tub and covered with a sack and allowed to cool. But before this, take a little of the warm beer in a basin, add two ounces of yeast and let it stand for the night. Add this to the main tub in the morning, then cask the beer. You can drink it after a week. And it won't be like anything you can taste at the Crown, either.

Just the same, he was almost certainly at the Crown after nightfall. Where else to find merry companionship?

When Julius Caesar took over Britain in 55 B.C., he complained rudely that because it didn't grow grapes, the only drink he could find was metheglin, or mead, which he called "rain-water and honey, sodden together."

The Britons didn't invent mead. It had been around since the dawn of time, wherever there were bees. Norse gods and heroes in Valhalla gave it credit for all wisdom and poetry. On Mount Olympus it was the nectar of the gods we hear so much about, and the bees that made it were sacred to Demeter, goddess of agriculture. In classical Greek the word for "drunk" means overcome by honey. In India a collection of Hindu Sanskrit hymns tells us that "In the wide-striding Vishnu's highest footsteps there is a Spring of Mead," and if you could find and drink it, your fertility would burgeon and sons would result. Especially since mead was considered an aphrodisiac and the best way to seduce virgins.

In monasteries, monks busied their days with making it. In Poland it was so essential to life that the Polish prince told the pope that Poles couldn't possibly fight in the Crusades, since there wasn't any mead in the Holy Lands. In Sweden and Finland mead spiced with lemon is still the essential drink for Walpurgis Night, the spring fertility festival. Saxons, as attested by the disaster in *Beowulf,* considered it sissy to quit drinking mead while you could still speak. As Thomas Love Peacock put it a thousand years later,

> *He is not drunk who from the floor*
> *Can rise again and drink some more,*
> *But he is drunk who prostrate lies*
> *And cannot drink and cannot rise.*

Lacking taverns in feudal times, the lord of the manor built in his big house an enormous mead-hall, the bigger the better, and here the tenants and serfs and neighbors repaired in the evenings and the lord served forth unlimited mead, in return for their love, and loyalty and rent and their arms in battle against the neighboring lord, and everyone drank his fill.

America is currently eager to see drinking as a highly specialized field of expertise, a job for professionals, rather than vulgar fun. To this end we stupefy everyone with our knowledge of vintages and microbreweries, and use the word "artisanal" a lot. The more historical and authentic we can get, the better we feel about our expertise, whatever it tastes like.

Last fall I found an artisanal meaderie in an old log cabin deep in central Virginia. The proprietor did indeed look like a fugitive from a time warp, but his time seemed closer to 1968 than 55 B.C. He was friendly and cheerful, with long unkempt locks and a following of dogs and cats. Sweet pastoral innocence hovered over the place and its woods and fields, far from those crowded halls packed with brawling feudal retainers.

My friend and I were the only visitors; we'd come at the wrong time of year. Mead, proper mead, is obviously a summer project, needing bees and a variety of flowers, each with its own flavor (the honeysuckle was highly recommended). Now, though, as he prepared for his winter occupation of making dulcimers, he had only a few bottles left, of a generic flavor.

We tasted. To palates tuned to Scotch and vodka, it was sweetish. Hard to imagine our ancestors pouring it down all night long without throwing up, but then maybe they did throw up, the better to drink some more.

We bought several of his last bottles. He apologized that they had no labels; he printed all the labels by hand and he'd run out of them. I carried mine home and tried unsuccessfully to give it to people for Christmas. The bottle was tall and skinny and certainly, unlabeled, it looked sinister. My sister said dubiously that she might cook something with it, but I said I didn't think so.

Curiously, nobody discussing those Herculean bouts of yore mentions the hangover, and our ancestors didn't even have a word for it. The *Oxford English Dictionary,* lordly arbiter of our language, doesn't list it in its main text, but it does offer an appendix, or afterthought, including questionable new usages and lowly Americanisms. Here we find "hangover," a purely American word that didn't appear in print until 1894. It means "a thing or person remaining or left over; a remainder or survival."

Samuel Pepys in the seventeenth century does confess to waking up with his "head in a sad taking through last night's drink," but a friend persuades him to treat it with a very stiff, medical-grade chocolate along with his usual breakfast booze, and he goes off to the naval office without benefit of Alka-Seltzer. Apparently most of our ancestors greeted the dawn with a tankard of beer or a jolt of brandy, or both, and what was once called the "hair of the dog that bit you" restored the blood sugar and slowed the sickening drop of the blood-alcohol level. The modern hangover may be attributed partly to our stern morning sobriety and partly to guilt: we're being punished, and we deserve it. Our ancestors in the mead-hall felt pretty guiltless about their consumption. Indeed, they were proud of it.

Mead was a sturdy addition to the diet. Medicinal herbs were stored in metheglin to preserve them over the winter, and fruits and berries could be added to it for a few winter vitamins. The word "honeymoon" comes, they say, from the custom of the bride's father giving the happy couple a month's supply of mead with which to cement their union.

It might be that some honey doesn't even need fermenting. Paul Salopek, writing in a recent issue of *National Geographic,* says the Pygmies deep in Congo are enraptured by their wild rain-forest honey to the point of obsession. They smoke a bit of marijuana, but only to fight fatigue; for fun they eat honey. He goes with them on a successful honey hunt; they stuff themselves in an orgy of liquid gold. The men wax rowdy, shouting and arguing, the women tell dirty jokes and roar with laughter, the children shriek and roister around in the trees with the hives, dribbling honey down their chins. Trying it, Salopek calls the stuff unforgettable: "It goes quickly to the head, its delicious perfume carries with it the suggestion of a better world. As it seeps directly from the membranes of the mouth into the bloodstream, yielding up its concentrated energy, generously radiating its stored warmth, a single word comes to mind: Yes."

What more can Napoleon brandy offer? Why bother to learn to process such a ready-made pleasure?

The Romans, disgusted with mead, tried to civilize the Britons with wine. Grapeless, they made apple wine and hard cider, which proved quite alarmingly popular but didn't replace the more usual brews. By the sixth century the Romans had gone home and British monks and nuns were causing rather a scandal by being too full of ale to function.

Mead still flourished. In the tenth century, the saintly King Edward the Martyr, "a vessel full of every virtuous grace," had a wicked stepmother, Elfrida, who thought her own son Ethelred should be king instead. When Edward rode up to the castle for a visit, before he could get off his horse she rushed out to greet him with a goodly mug of mead, which he could hardly refuse. While he was slugging it down, her henchman came up behind him and stabbed him in the back. He fell off his horse, dead, and Ethelred was king.

In 1066 the Normans stormed in, bringing plenty of their own French wine. They found the locals uncouth. The Norman William of Malmesbury, in his *History of the Kings of England,* wrote that at the time of the conquest, "Drinking in particular was a universal practice, in which occupation they passed entire nights as well as days . . . They were accustomed to eat till they became surfeited and drink till they were sick."

He had the grace to add that the invaders lost no time in taking up the local customs.

William the Conqueror, they say, some twenty years after the invasion, finding himself too fat to ride his horse, took to his bed and followed a strict all-alcohol diet. How much weight he lost isn't recorded, but since he later died when his horse fell down, at least he'd been able to get onto the creature, though maybe he was too drunk to stay there, or perhaps his bulk brought it to its knees. We can't recommend his drinks-only regime to modern dieters, however, since it was recorded that his corpse was so bulky the attendant clergy had a lot of trouble wedging it into his stone sarcophagus and by the time they succeeded the whole place smelled just awful.

His son William Rufus, blundering around the New Forest, got himself killed by a stray arrow. It was said he'd been "soothing his cares with an unusual quantity of wine." In eleventh-century Britain, an unusual quantity was a lot.

Vineyards had been planted to slake the thirst of the Norman nobility and clergy. As always, certain drinks favored by the upper classes were considered unwholesome for the masses. Wycliffe's fourteenth-century translation of the Bible warned, "For he schal be gret before the Lord, and he schal not drink wyn ni cyder." The upper clergy didn't feel this applied to them, and some of the fancier medieval wines were given names like Bishop, Cardinal, and Pope. For festive events like coronations, wine poured freely from every conduit in town for days. Special fountains were designed for special occasions, gushing forth white wine from one side and red from the other.

For everyday nourishment, though, beer and ale reigned in Britain and Northern Europe. Hadn't Ireland's beloved St. Brigid changed her bathwater into beer to refresh a traveling clergyman? And in families high and low, babies were weaned on beer, always ready to hand, wholesome, and far safer than unpasteurized, unrefrigerated milk from unsterilized bottles.

Even the doughtiest conquerors give up, assimilate, and drink local. Scarcely a hundred years after William Rufus died of complications of wine, Bad King John was said to have died from a surfeit of "new ale."

Beer was made with hops, a relative of marijuana with an interesting strong, bitter flavor and preservative qualities, and ale was made without hops, using assorted other flavorings, anything from pepper to honey. John's ale had to have been new, since it only kept for two weeks, but maybe it wasn't new enough. Or maybe it was a peculiarly powerful batch, since killing yourself with ale at a single sitting would take a prodigious stomach. Or maybe the barkeep added a little something off the menu: John wasn't popular.

In winter, and especially around the extreme merriment of the long Christmas, hot drinks were served freely, hot posset and apple ale and wassail. Samuel Johnson's 1756 dictionary says wassail is "a liquor made of apples, sugar, and ale; a drunken bout; a merry song." All three definitions combined happily.

Toasts were drunk. For ages, a party would include only one goblet for the whole table, passed from hand to hand. The polite drinker wiped his mouth first, then emptied the glass and passed it on, symbol of sharing and friendship. As table settings expanded and each got his own, it was polite to clink your glass against your neighbors', meaning that we're still all sharing the same stuff; we're still friends and equals. We lifted the glass to drink good health to the next man, who drank our health in turn, and eventually everyone else's, including absent friends; royalty actual, exiled, or deposed; pretty women; and anyone else that came to mind. It could get competitive, as no man durst admit himself toasted out until he fell down unconscious.

Our classical barfly was Shakespeare's Falstaff, he of the great belly, drinker, jester, and singer, who led young Prince Hal into low company. He was a regular at the Boar's Head Tavern, where he molested the womenfolk and drank enormous quantities of sack.

Sack was a sweet, amber-colored wine imported from Spain, sometimes called "sherris sack," being an ancestor of sherry, from the Spanish province of Jerez. The English "sack" seems to be a corruption of *vin sec,* or dry wine, though it could have beaten the socks off your Chardonnay with one hand tied behind it.

Falstaff feels sack essential to wit, intelligence, manliness, and the army:

There's never none of these demure boys come to any proof; for thin drink doth so over-cool their blood, and making many fish meals, that they fall into a kind of male green-sickness . . . They are generally fools and cowards . . . A good sherris-sack hath a two-fold operation in it. It ascends me into the brain; dries me there all the foolish and dull and crudy vapours which environ it; makes it apprehensive, quick, forgetive, full of nimble, fiery, and delectable shapes which, delivered o'er to the voice, the tongue, which is the birth, becomes excellent wit. The second property of your excellent sherris is the warming of the blood; which, before cold and settled, left the liver white and pale, which is the badge of pusillanimity and cowardice; but the sherris warms it and makes it course from the inwards to the parts extreme: it illumineth the face, which as a beacon, gives warning to all the rest of this little kingdom, man, to arm . . . So that skill in the weapon is nothing without sack, for that sets it a-work; and learning a mere hoard of gold kept by a devil, till sack commences it and sets it in act and use.

It was all the fine sack he poured down Prince Hal that made a man of him.

Hereof comes it that Prince Harry is valiant; for the cold blood he did naturally inherit of his father he hath, like lean, sterile, and bare land, manured, husbanded, and tilled, with excellent endeavour of drinking good, and good store of fertile sherris, that he has become very hot and valiant.

His advice to parents: "If I had a thousand sons, the first humane principle I would teach them should be to forswear thin potations, and to addict themselves to sack."

British manhood and even the safety of the country depended on strong drink; a soldier who drank weak drinks was too weak for battle.

When the old king dies, Falstaff is delighted. With his good drinking buddy on the throne, he himself will become a power in the land, seated beside the new king, keeping him larky and happy: "O, you shall see him laugh till his face be like a wet cloak ill laid up."

Alas, with the crown barely settled on his head, Prince Hal turns prig. He casts off all his old habits and merry companions, presumably drinking only springwater and eating broccoli. He tells Falstaff, "I know thee not," and banishes him "not to come near our person by ten mile" until he can prove that he, too, has reformed.

Instead of reforming, Falstaff holes up in the Boar's Head and dies, we're told, of a broken heart, or perhaps a surfeit of sack. But afterward young Henry V proved how true his teacher had been in the matter of fighting spirit. After so many years of good sack, his courage survived his abstinence and he won many a splendid battle.

Coffee had landed in the Old World, and coffeehouses sprang up to challenge the taverns. The authorities were suspicious of the whole thing and sent spies to eavesdrop. In the taverns all was amiable and easy, but the coffeehouses were cauldrons of edgy malcontents, alert and angry, hatching plots against the state.

Besides, coffee was new, unsanctified by tradition, and

probably weakened the flesh. In 1674, in London, a group of women got together to protest and published a pamphlet called "Women's Petition against COFFEE, Representing to Publick Consideration the Grand INCOVENIENCIES Accruing to Their SEX from the Excessive Use of that Drying, Enfeebling LIQUOR." They maintained that England was supposed to be paradise for women, but such "can consist in nothing more than the brisk *Activity* of our men, who in former ages were justly esteemed the *Ablest Performers* in Christendome." Now, alas, their old vigor was so decayed that they couldn't perform their marital duties, "The Occasion of which Insufferable *Disaster . . .* we can Attribute to nothing more than the Excessive use of that Newfangled, Abominable, Heathenish Liquor called *COF- FEE,* which Riffling Nature of her Choicest *Treasures,* and *Drying* up the *Radical Moisture,* has so *Eunucht* our Husbands and *Crippled* our more kind *Gallants,* that they are become as *Impotent* as Age, and as unfruitful as those *Desarts* whence that unhappy *Berry* is said to be brought."

No amount of blandishment can rouse these enfeebled, dry, and sapless coffee drinkers. They have forsaken "the good old primitive way of Ale-drinking to run a *whoreing* after such variety of destructive *Foreign* Liquors, to . . . scald their *Chops* and spend their *Money,* all for a little *base, black, thick, nasty, bitter, stinking, nauseous* Puddle-water." They urge the authorities to ban coffee for all men under sixty and promote the drinking of "*Lusty nappy beer, Cock- Ale, Cordial Canaries,*" so that women may have their rights and privileges restored and "That our Husbands may give us some other *Testimonies* of their being Men besides their *Beards* and wearing of empty *Pantaloons.*"

We don't know whether the current inhabitants of

Starbucks are aware of this problem, but they're probably too busy for sex anyway.

Coffee didn't really replace ale until far in the future. Kings and clergymen, peasants and students rejoiced in their taverns. For as long as there have been universities, right up until yesterday, the tavern was the heart and soul of university life. Here the students gathered around the pitcher of beer to argue, debate, philosophize, forge lifelong bonds, and sing rude traditional songs handed down through generations. When they looked back, the graduates considered that tavern, university, and friends were all one and the same. Perhaps most of the underpinnings of modern literature, science, religion, and philosophy were hammered out around a table full of wine bottles or beer steins. Perhaps most of the participants were under twenty-one.

After various states had passed their own laws, in 1984 in America it became federal law that nobody under twenty-one could drink anything stronger than Coca-Cola. Now America's youth can vote, marry, have children, and get sent off in uniform to die for their country three long years before they can legally pop a cold beer on a hot afternoon.

A hundred or so years earlier, many states had had their own drinking-age laws making it illegal to sell, at least publicly, strong spirits to anyone under the age of ten. Other states didn't care. I hear that the United Kingdom is currently the only country to impose a minimum drinking age in the home, age five, but only with parental consent.

Virtuous college students now retreat to their rooms

and play computer games alone, while the unvirtuous bribe an older friend to buy them a bottle of vodka, which they glug down in the parking lot. Some die. Neither friendship nor philosophy is served. Cars were the culprit. For a thousand years, a youth with too many beers under his belt might fall off a horse or stumble into a ditch or need help from his friends getting back to the dorm, but he rarely killed anyone on his way. With fast wheels under him, he turned into a deadly weapon.

A noble and ancient tradition fell prey to Ford's contraption.

Back to history. Henry VIII could down a tankard or three with the best of them, as one can plainly see from his portraits, and his daughter Elizabeth carried on the tradition. Her court was more decorous than his—his right-hand cleric, Cardinal Wolsey, had been clapped in the stocks for public drunkenness in his younger days—but all her ladies-in-waiting drank beer for breakfast, and she took a serious interest in her drink. At home she had her own brew, "so strong as there was no man able to drink it," but when she traveled around the country visiting, the local products fell short in both strength and quantity. Wrote the Earl of Leicester to Lord Burleigh, "There is not one drop of good drink here for her. We were fain to send to London, and Kenilworth, and divers other places where ale was."

Elizabeth knew a thing or two about brewing and kept a close eye on the brewers. She cracked down hard on them for overcharging and for delivering their product when it was only two or three hours old: all beer, she decreed, must stand in the brewer's house for six hours in summer and eight in winter before being sold.

There are many fine rumors about Shakespeare whooping it up in the Mermaid Tavern with his fellow poets. Certainly he was a good member of its Friday Street Club, along with Sir Walter Raleigh, John Donne, Ben Jonson, and other literary notables, of whom Keats much later wrote:

> *Souls of poets dead and gone,*
> *What Elysium have ye known,*
> *Happy field or mossy cavern,*
> *Choicer than the Mermaid Tavern?*
> *Have ye tippled drink more fine*
> *Than mine host's Canary wine?*

Close scrutiny seems to show, though, that Will just wasn't much of a drinker by the standards of the day. A weak stomach, perhaps, like his Cassio's and Stephano's? Indeed, he may not have quite approved of drinking, at least in immoderation: Falstaff is a buffoon, Sir Toby Belch is a loser, and Hamlet speaks out quite priggishly against his country's "heavy-headed revel." Plenty of people drank too much at the Mermaid, but the Bard may have surreptitiously poured his into a potted plant.

James, Elizabeth's successor, was Scottish and less enthusiastic about English traditions. In fact, he was against drunkenness as undermining the manual trades, and he imposed a fine of five shillings or six hours in the stocks for going around pie-eyed.

His rules, like most such, were intended to keep the working man in shape to keep working, and did not apply to the higher sort of folk. Indeed, London seemed to be drinking more than ever, and James himself is rumored to have been foremost among them, having picked up the habit from his nurse in his isolated Scottish childhood. Marriage to Anne of Denmark didn't help, since the Danes were strict in their drinking rules, everyone in the group had to drink a separate toast to everyone else in the group, however large the gathering: forty guests meant thirty-nine drinks drained to the last drop. At the Stuarts' even the most formal royal ceremonies sometimes got out of hand.

James's son, Charles I, was actually a far soberer and more virtuous character, but the Puritans had been sulking and muttering for several reigns now and suddenly decided it was their turn to run things, rose up in rebellion, cut off his head, and installed Oliver Cromwell. They called him The Protector, since God sent him to protect the people from their baser natures.

We all think of the Puritans as a prissy bunch of fanatics, but national habits die hard and actually they managed to put away plenty of good English ale between prayer meetings. Under an early version of the blue laws, Cromwell's henchmen also made a bundle out of snooping around on Sundays and fining everyone they found selling or downing a Sabbath drink. Nevertheless a French visitor during the Puritan reign marveled at the number of alehouses, so that half the population, he said, seemed to be tavern keepers and even the ladies of quality hung out in pubs, drinking with the best.

Cromwell's death, according to the diarist John Evelyn, was "the joyfullest funeral I ever saw, for there were none that cried but dogs," and the whole country got drunk to welcome Charles II, another merry old hard-drinking Stuart. As Daniel Defoe wrote later, "Very merry, and very mad, and very drunken, the people were, and grew more and more so every day." Brandy, mostly imported from France, flowed freely.

Some busybody dug up the domestic expenses of a presumably typical family during Charles II's reign. There were seven in the family, ages not recorded but certainly some infants or toddlers, and every week they drank thirty-six gallons of beer, or about three quarts a day apiece. This was only the household consumption. How much more they downed in the local tavern is anyone's guess.

On top of all that beer, considered more food than drink, French and Spanish wines and brandy were put away by the barrelful. Laws kept the prices down and people drank so freely of the imports that the government worried about the flow of money to foreign vineyards. Even Charles noticed that his subjects were making pretty merry, and he issued a stern rebuke to men "who spend their time in taverns, tippling houses, and debauches, giving no other evidence of their affection to us but in drinking our health." This description probably covered his entire circle of friends, relatives, ministers, courtiers, naval officers, employees, and assorted hangers-on, but there's no evidence that anyone paid the least attention. Though the diarist Samuel Pepys was one of the most responsible and dutiful civil servants of the era and actually showed up for work, he, too, spent much of his days and nights and even mornings emptying bowls and tankards with the best of them. Indeed, the wonder was that, with such yeoman consumption all over, anyone stayed upright long enough to keep the country going.

Charles II was replaced by his brother, James II, who was so grossly unattractive that the country, exasperated, threw him out and replaced him with his daughter Mary and her husband, William of Orange. William was Dutch and brought along with him his personal favorite drink, gin, of which he drank immoderately. He passed it on to the populace.

Gin Lane

Riot and slaughter once again
Shall their career begin,
And every parish suckling babe
Again be nursed with Gin.

—18TH-CENTURY STREET SONG

IN EUROPE IN THE late Middle Ages, the distillers' art seeped in as a secret formula, the alchemists transforming gentle wine into something fierce and mystical, the water of life, aqua vitae, either the wonder drug that cured everything from palsy to plague or possibly the black arts of the devil, or both.

Light a fire under the wine-filled still and vapors rise to its narrow neck, condense, and dribble forth as the powerful new medicine. *Alcohol* comes from the Arabic word meaning "sweat," that magical drip of the condensed vapors. From secret mixes of herbs, exotic smells and tastes emerged. *The Treasury of Euonymous* lists, among other ingredients, rue, sage, lavender, marjoram, wormwood, rosemary, red roses, thistle, pimpernel, valerian, juniper berries, bay leaves, angelica, citrus bark, coriander, sandalwood, basil, grain of paradise, pepper, ginger, cinnamon, mace, nutmeg, and cardamom. The sixteenth-century pharmacist/bartender had whole libraries of secret recipes. Some of the ingredients were considered medicinal, but a lot of them were just to mask the ferocious flavor of the drink as it came from the still. The licorice taste of anise was always useful, hiding even the bitter wormwood of absinthe and echoing down through Greek ouzo, Turkish raki, Italian *sambuca,* and French pastis.

The alcohol was the base, but the magical spices were the selling point. As a major player in the spice trade, Holland sat firmly on the new science. Distilleries trumped windmills, wooden shoes, and tulips; by the 1570s the Bols gin-works near Amsterdam was flourishing. Juniper was the favored flavoring, and gin was originally "Geneva," from the French for juniper, *genievre.*

Presently it turned out that the fierce new medicine didn't cure bubonic plague after all, but doctors recommended it for most other problems, physical and mental. One medical man wrote, "it sharpeneth the wit" and "it maketh me merry and preserveth youth." The military praised its effect on men in battle: "Dutch courage." During the Dutch war of the mid-1600s, Daniel Defoe wrote that "the captains of the Hollanders' Men of War, when they were to engage with our ships, usually set a hogshead of brandy abroach, afore the mast, and bid the men drink lustick, then they might fight lustick; and our poor seamen felt the force of the brandy, sometimes to their cost."

The magical distillation spread far and wide, to general rejoicing. Brandy sprang from the wines of France. Whiskey rose out of the grains of Ireland and Scotland, and in Edinburgh a bell rang daily at noon to remind everyone to down the essential midday half cup of whiskey that—along with other cupfuls at other times—inspired the great writers and inventors of the Scottish Enlightenment.

The potatoes of Russia turned into vodka. Russian gentry drank a lot of champagne; Peter the Great, after an evening's merrymaking, always carried four bottles of it up to bed with him, but this didn't mean he scorned the national lifeblood. On the contrary, he had a special vessel that held a liter and a half of vodka and prospective diplomats had to prove they could down it in a single draft and still talk sense. The same test was laid on foreign diplomats come to court; the results often tilted affairs in favor of the seasoned Russians.

Gin was the drink of Germany, the Netherlands, and England. It was much easier to make than drinkable brandy or whiskey; if you didn't have a regular supply of wine, almost anything else could be distilled instead, including common and plentiful wheat, rye, oats, or barley. It was cheap. It packed a wallop quite different from beer and wine, being usually from 100 to 160 proof.

When it came to England some considered gin unnatural and even ungodly. Long, long ago the good Lord had given mankind the gentle convivial blessings of mead, beer, and wine, the comradely taverns where a man could spend a long merry evening with friends and still walk home. The new stuff was drunk more privately, even furtively, and quickly. As it came out of the still it was much stronger than our modern diluted versions, delivering its punch of release from care and leaving the drinker in a sodden heap within the hour.

The manly alehouse had discouraged women, but

strong spirits were available everywhere, unconstrained by tradition, and the weaker sex joined the party. One medical man complained that in the past, a gently alcoholic cordial would cure most women's ailments, but now "many English women have betaken themselves to the drinking of brandy and other spirits, and have invented the black-cherry brandy, which is in great esteem, so that she is nobody that hath not a bottle of it at her elbow." Any little qualm, real or fancied, he said, and it's "away to the brandy bottle." This is a problem for the doctors, because their old remedies fall pretty flat after all that brandy. (We're talking about nice women here, of course, not the back-alley gin-drinkers who wouldn't have known a doctor from a doorknob.)

William's first royal step was to declare war on France and cut off the imports of French brandy. This was hard on the French and, even better, left a vacuum in the drinks world to be filled with local product, particularly gin distilled from good English grain crops. With negligible taxes, it was wonderfully cheap. Without the web of ancient regulations surrounding beer, anyone could make it and anyone with a back door could sell it to all comers. It met with enthusiasm.

Particularly in London. Londoners made it out of whatever came to hand, flavored it with the traditional juniper berries, and called it Geneva. By 1720, someone guessed, two and a half million gallons a year were made and mostly drunk by six hundred thousand Londoners. In some quarters, one out of every five households kept busy cooking it up. Tradesmen and shopkeepers passed it out on credit to their employees who, having roistered during the week's work, had nothing left to collect on payday.

One report protested that there was no way to count the sources, since "'tis known there are many others who sell by retail . . . in the streets . . . some on bulks and stalls set up for that purpose, and others in wheelbarrows . . . and many more who sell privately in garrets, cellars, back rooms, and other places." Vendors with nothing more than "a tray, a bottle, and a couple of dirty glasses" stood on every street corner. Much of it must have been nasty and sometimes downright poisonous, but it all packed the essential wallop.

Visiting foreigners sometimes observed that it was necessary for the natives to drink lots of strong spirits in order to survive the English climate, but most complained that they could barely navigate the London streets, strewn as they were with drunks of all ages. Little girls took up prostitution to support their habit. In 1751 the novelist Henry Fielding, who was also a magistrate, wrote:

> A new kind of drunkenness, unknown to our ancestors, is lately sprung up amongst us, which, if not put a stop to, will infallibly destroy a great part of the inferior people. The drunkenness I here intend is that acquired by the strongest intoxicating liquors, and particularly by that poison called Gin, which, I have great reason to think, is the principal sustenance (if it may be so called) of more than a hundred thousand people in the Metropolis. Many of these wretches there are, who swallow pints of this poison within the twenty-four hours, the dreadful effects of which I have the misfortune every day to see, and to smell too.

As he says, the victims were "inferior people." Strong drink, like education, was too much for the proletariat to handle. The problem, as always, was how much the working classes could drink and still keep working.

London's upper classes were dedicated to port instead, a far more genteel tipple that took all evening to do its job. For those who worked at all, the working day was only about four hours long, so plenty of time remained for port. Dinner was served in mid-afternoon, and after it the ladies withdrew to the withdrawing room and the men sat around the dinner table till midnight.

A gentleman might put away, in the course of this leisurely social bonding, four to six bottles of port, drunk slowly in small glassfuls, and take a fresh bottle up to bed with him. Back then, port wasn't sweet and, like sherry, had brandy added to it to increase its muscle. A French winemakers' newspaper complained that the English had ruined their palates "by drinking spirits and strong beer. Consequently they find our wines, the chief merit of which consists in the finesse and delicacy of the bouquet, too light. What they want is something that is rough, strong, and catches in the throat . . . the stronger the better." So that's what the French sent them.

Though he might need to be pulled from under the table and put to bed, the gentleman was ready to do it all over again the next night and none thought the worse of him.

William of Orange went out riding, possibly far from sober, and his horse tripped over a mole run, plunging the king to his death. Everyone who wanted the Stuarts back on the throne drank toasts to the horse, whose name was Sorrel, and to the mole, whose name they didn't know, so they drank, "Health and long life to the Little Gentleman in Velvet!"

They did get another Stuart, Queen Anne, but she wasn't very merry. Quite dismal, in fact. After eighteen pregnancies, all her children were dead and she consoled herself so copiously that her loyal subjects called her "Dram Shop" and "Brandy Nan" for her "well-known liking for the bottle and spirituous liquors," and in those days it was hard work to get famous for drinking.

She died, to be followed by various Georges.

Drinking for the upper classes was an after-dinner sport. (Beer and ale didn't count as drinking; they were basic to the menu: roast meat, bread, beer.) The pre-dinner drink arose in Sweden in the seventeenth century, aquavit, served with bread, cheese, and herring. It spread to France as the French convinced themselves that a large glass of vermouth, absinthe, or brandy was an essential preparation of the stomach for the savoring of the food and wines to come.

And in the sprawling London slums gin was drunk morning, noon, and night, without reference to food, by people with no table manners.

Overworked magistrates complained. The doctors, former fans of gin as medicine, now claimed that gin made the lower classes "diseas'd, not fit for business, poor, and a burthen to themselves and neighbours, and too often the cause of weak, feeble, and distemper'd children, who must be, instead of an advantage and strength, a charge to their country." All around the gentlemen the lower orders, though mostly out of sight, were coming unstuck with gin and lying down on the job.

Daniel Defoe had praised gin mostly as a mainstay of

the economy, but two years later he changed his mind, saying that the way to make London great was "to save our lower class of people from utter ruin, and rendering them useful by preventing the immoderate use of Geneva." The new King George publicly deplored the nonworking state of London's workers. Puritanical types complained that gin led to blasphemy and adultery. Gentlemen complained that, drunk, the masses forgot their proper station in life and thought they were as good as anyone.

Parliament was forced to take notice. Clearly the price was the problem. The right sort of people could afford to get drunk on the genteel fluids they were entitled to, but if the poor could, as advertisers claimed, get drunk for a penny, no wonder gin was "the bane of the vulgar." The price would need to be raised out of their vulgar reach.

Parliament piously proclaimed that the drinking of spirits "is become very common among the people of inferior rank . . . greatly to the destruction of their healths, enervating them, and rendering them unfit for useful labour and service." It decreed a retail license on gin sellers of twenty pounds a year, probably more than they made, so the lower orders would get sober and the king would get rich.

It didn't work. The excise men sent out to collect the fees were trying to track down thousands of nameless retailers in thousands of unlabeled London sheds, cellars, and kitchens. They were chased and threatened. Probably slop buckets were emptied on their heads.

Another trouble was defining gin. The law said it was spirits with "juniper berries, or other fruit, spices, or ingredients." Fair enough: leave out the trimmings and sell the raw spirits unprocessed. They called it "Parliamentary

Brandy," and it was foul, fiery, and toxic. A year after the Gin Act of 1729, consumption was back up to four and a half million gallons, and its devotees were filling the hospitals and almshouses.

Landowners complained of the shrunken grain market, since the homemade spirits weren't necessarily made of grain. The year's crops had been excessively bountiful and, if not made into gin, they'd rot. Besides, the income from the act had been disappointing, since fees and fines were rarely collected. In 1733 a new act repealed the tax, but added that street vendors couldn't openly carry a tray around selling drams and impeding foot traffic. To sell gin now, you had to keep a roof over its head.

The reformers raged. "How often," they cried, "do we see women lying in the very channels and corners of streets like dead carcasses, generally without cloaths to protect them from the inclemency of the weather, or cover their nakedness and shame? How many breaches of the peace, dangerous assaults, and often murders have been occasion'd by this deluge of debauchery?" Others pointed out that servants of both sexes, drunk, became ever less reliable, often quite unable to carry out their duties, and "are frequently seen on our streets, in a condition abhorrent to reasonable creatures." "Dutch courage" had failed: even the once-stalwart British foot soldier, defender of the empire, now lay in a sodden heap. Thousands of new gin shops opened.

Then Parliament passed a bill for the "total suppression of all distilled spirituous liquors." Terrorists set off a bomb in Westminster in protest. Mobs howled in the streets. Dark plots were uncovered. Guards were doubled all over London, a number of people got drunk in mourning and several, unable to face the future, committed suicide. "Mother Gin" was ceremoniously buried in effigy. A broadside entitled "An Elegy on the Much Lamented Death of the Most Excellent, the Most Truly-Beloved, and Universally-Admired Lady, Madame Gineva," sneered at the mourners: "Unhappy Briton! More enslaved than Turk, forc'd to be sober and compelled to work!" Work, as everyone knew, was the only salvation of the lower orders, as leisure was their certain ruination.

Nobody really expected the ban to last. Of the perhaps ten thousand gin peddlers in London, only two applied that winter for the fifty-pound licenses. Old women with baskets, mom-and-pop stores, and market stalls peddled products creatively labeled Cuckold's Comfort, Make Shift, the Ladies' Delight, Kill-Grief, and Gripe Water. The magistrates labored and packed the jails but it was hopeless, and many citizens worked the streets before dawn brazenly selling plain gin from unmarked jugs carried under their cloaks or skirts.

The Gin Act didn't cause the expected riots and rebellions, but it didn't cause much else either, except bootleggers. Dudley Bradstreet (if that was his real name; much of his résumé was invented) was the Al Capone of London. He got a friend to take a house in Blue Anchor Alley, where he put up a sign of a cat in the window and spread word that "gin would be sold by the cat at my window." He spent his last money on some really good gin and rigged a pipe under the cat's paw: put tuppence into the cat's mouth, and lo, tuppence worth of gin came out of the pipe.

Word spread, and the customers clogged the alley. Neighbors complained. There were no police as we think of them now, and anyway the constables were busy selling gin themselves. Cat copycats sprang up all over: step in and call "Puss!" and a voice answers "Mew!" and a drawer shoots out; put your money in the drawer and it's pulled inside and reappears with gin.

It wasn't exactly martini quality. A contemporary wrote that, being illegal, it was now made not so much from malt as from "rotten fruit, urine, lime, human ordure, and any other filthiness from whence a fermentation may be raised, and by throwing in cochylus indice and other hot poisonous drugs." Turpentine was the most popular flavoring. Sulfuric acid was added for its kick. Nobody counted the customers who went blind or dropped dead.

The authorities offered rewards to informers, but the citizens roughed up informers pretty brutally. When one man threatened to kill a lady informer, he was thrown into Newgate Prison and his friends started a genuine riot, over a thousand outraged citizens milling and shouting in front of the justice's house. The justice read them the Riot Act, requiring them to disperse, but they dispersed not. Finally the army was called in to clear the street.

Convicted gin dealers, three-quarters of them women, were snatched on their way to prison by angry crowds and carried off to safety. Informers, many also women, banded together in gangs; the leader of one gang was credited with turning in four thousand retailers at five pounds apiece, and the magistrates began to smell a rat.

During the seven years the Gin Act was enforced, the production of spirituous liquors increased by over a third, enough for every man, woman, and small child in London to put away a quart a week on top of their beer.

And the government wasn't making a penny off it.

Realists wanted it legalized and the taxes set high enough so that at least London's low-class wives and mothers couldn't afford it. The moralists howled, but the pragmatists won, and in 1743 the ban was lifted and licenses, more modestly priced, were issued to legitimate taverns.

In 1748 the war with Spain was over, and seventy thousand servicemen were thrown out of work, spearheading a wave of robberies and muggings. Respectable folk went out only by daylight and heavily armed. Gin took the blame.

In 1751 Hogarth published his famous print, *Gin Lane.* The central figure in this busy street scene is a woman, catatonically drunk, sitting at the top of a steep flight of stairs with a baby slipping off her lap, about to plunge to its death. She is "Madame Geneva" herself, far more horrifying than a man in similar disarray. All around her, people are pawning their pots and pans and clothes for more gin, dishing out gin to groups of schoolchildren, murdering each other, and in general slowing the progress of the ship of state and undermining that hardworking docility so essential to the comfort of the better sort of folk. A sign over a shop advertises, "Drunk for a Penny, dead drunk for twopence, clean straw for Nothing." The straw was for sleeping it off.

Gin Lane's companion piece was *Beer Street,* where the good citizens, quaffing their wholesome ancestral beverage, are tidy, peaceful, and industrious.

Then the grain harvest failed and bread was in short supply. Parliament quickly passed yet another act, this time forbidding all distilling of spirits from grains until the crisis passed, but it was four years before the sun came out and the harvest came back. In the meantime, the reformers rejoiced. With nothing to drink, one wrote, the lower classes "at once became sober, industrious, vigorous, hardy, brave, and governable."

Indeed, middle-class respectability was in the air. It swelled and spread, and formerly irresponsible folk began taking their families for picnics instead of swilling gin in the alleys. A progressive spirit peered into the land and some went so far as to suggest that the poor and wretched were drinking because they were poor and wretched instead of being poor and wretched because they drank.

Distillers that had managed to survive the ban went industrial. Gordon and Booth and Tanqueray were well-known names by the end of the 1700s. Housewives and corner grocery stores no longer made their own.

In the outposts of the British Empire, the colonials were urged to take quinine to help prevent malaria. In the 1870s Schweppes produced the first fizzy quinine water familiarly known as tonic, and it went down nicely with lashings of gin. After the empire dissolved, returning colonials brought it home. Hence the refreshing summer standby of garden parties, with its cool jingle of ice and cheerful slice of lime, a world away from the tuppenny drunks in the slums of yore. The well-chilled martini became the iconic drink of important people everywhere.

Socially, gin swooped up from the lowest gutters and took over the loftiest pinnacles. Perhaps ice made the difference. Well-chilled gin in a triangular glass isn't even a distant social cousin to the same stuff warm from a bottle.

Pilgrims' Problems

O they call it that old mountain dew,
And them that refuse it are few,
And I'll shut up my mug
If you'll fill up my jug
With that good old mountain dew.

—AMERICAN FOLK SONG

EARLY IN THE SEVENTEENTH CENTURY, England established a cluster of colonies on the eastern shore of North America, and various Britons came over, some cross and disaffected, some indentured or exiled, some pigheaded and righteous, and many simply hoping to get richer than they were back home. For a while, some hoped to persuade the natives to sell themselves into slavery and dig up gold for them, but the locals didn't take to slavery and there wasn't any gold, so some went back home and others hunkered down to make what they could of the place.

When the *Mayflower*'s Pilgrims landed on Plymouth Rock in 1620 they were already in serious beer trouble. They'd exhausted the supplies they'd brought along and started cadging off the ship's captain, but now the ship's own supplies were almost gone, and what would the crew drink on its way back home? Water doesn't keep well at sea and besides, it was considered at best unnourishing and at worst poisonous. And in case of sickness, beer, wine, or spirits were basic medicine; nobody recovered from anything without them.

The Pilgrims had brought a small amount of gin but not nearly enough, and they were far from home and about to be marooned here on this cold inhospitable shore. Governor William Bradford recorded bitterly that they "were hasted ashore and made to drink water, that the seamen might have the more beer." He pleaded with the ship, but the sailors were firm, saying that if "he were their own father, he should have none." Later the captain relented, but not by much.

Bradford sent back to England an order for two hogsheads of mead for his people and anxiously awaited the supply ship. When it showed up in 1630, only six gallons were left on board, the missing hundred gallons "being drunke up under ye name of leakage and so lost," he fumed.

The history books make much of the early settlers' troubles with food and shelter, but for many the drink problem was uppermost in mind. They were pleasantly surprised to find they could drink the New World's water without getting sick, but it was useful only for quenching thirst, not promoting health and strength.

The *Arabella* brought the Puritans to Boston in 1630, having prudently sailed with several times as much beer as water and ten thousand gallons of wine, but all things come to an end, and when would fresh supplies arrive from England, a long and expensive journey subject to "leakage"?

America's schoolchildren have been fed the vision of our early settlers as so virtuous they'd make your teeth hurt, and they were, they were. They just didn't connect sin with drinking. Their favorite commandment was the fourth, and they went to great lengths to make sure nobody had any fun on Sunday. God may have rested on the seventh day, but the Puritans' idea of rest was spending most of the day in church listening to hell-fire sermons, then sitting up very straight and silent reading the Bible, and no giggling.

God didn't get mixed up with alcohol for some hundreds of years to come. In fact, He was rather in favor of it, and the pious Puritan minister Increase Mather said, "Drink is in itself a good Creature of God, and to be received with thankfulness, but the abuse of drink is from Satan, the wine is from God, but the Drunkard is from the Devil." An early version of our incessant "moderation" sermons, with only a pint or two dividing heaven from hell.

The Pilgrims oiled their negotiations with Massasoit and other Indian leaders with generous bowlfuls of strong waters, probably brandy or Holland gin, and the chiefs kept coming back for more hospitality, bringing thirsty friends and relations, and signing on to any suggested scheme. By the time of the first Thanksgiving, the newcomers could offer their local guests white and red wines from the local wild grapes, said to be "very sweete & strong."

A rival colony sprang up to the north, where Quincy is

now, and dedicated itself to frivolity, scandalizing the Pilgrims by their "joylity." They could be heard singing and laughing and even seen dancing. Indians were invited to share their revels, though by this time it was pretty well established that Indians would "pawn their wits" for a drink. Everyone danced. Satan reigned. They partied with "riotous prodigality . . . quaffing and drinking both wine & strong waters in great excess." For our pious early colonists, drinking was fine, even necessary, as long as you didn't enjoy it. It was the godless fun of "Merie Mount" that bothered the righteous: it might be contagious. Others might start dancing.

The Pilgrims invaded the place, captured their leader, and shipped him back to England. The dancing ceased.

Over the 1630s and '40s the colonial population swelled, with perhaps seventy thousand newcomers, and though shipping was more frequent and heavily laden with casks and hogsheads of drink, it was clear that the new Americans needed to start making their own if they were going to survive.

The housewives rolled up their sleeves. The English beer they were weaned on was a dark and hefty brew of barley malt flavored with hops, about 6 percent alcohol, and almost any other drink would have been easier to make, but tradition is a sweet companion, especially in a strange land. They did their best. In the 1630s someone wrote:

If barley be wanting to make into malt,
We must be content and think it no fault,

For we can make liquor to sweeten our lips,
Of pumpkins and parsnips and walnut-tree chips.

In 1662 the governor of Connecticut succeeded in making beer out of corn, a triumph that got him elected to the Royal Society of London. It's been described as "palatable," but doesn't seem to have caught on.

The rich in New England and Virginia drank imported wines at considerable expense. One historian reports that "of these, fiery Madeiras were the favorite of all fashionable folk, and often each glass of wine was strengthened by a liberal dash of brandy." The British settlers, with no vineyard blood in their veins, didn't try to grow their own, but some French Huguenots in Virginia started planting vines until they realized tobacco was more profitable and ripped them out. Most people drank beer whenever they could get it. They went to great lengths to brew or import it. They longed for it. It was, well, it was home. It was the very soul of the hearth and health.

Then gradually it became evident that, tradition or no, beer wasn't the most efficient drink for a restless population in a big new country. As we wandered and explored and forged westward, we needed something that lasted longer and weighed less. Something, perhaps, with more of a kick for its bulk.

The first distillery was up and running on Staten Island by 1664, and Boston got its own three years later. Rum, brandy, and grain whiskey began to take over. (Gin was easy to make and strong as an ox, but slightly disreputable.) The colonists threw themselves into distilling. Good beer was a challenge, but good spirits came easily, and stills sprang up in the colonial backyards, welcoming peaches, pears, honey, corn, rye, apples, or potatoes.

The quality may have been uneven. When the good Quaker William Penn, a man who liked his comforts, landed in 1682 to start Pennsylvania, he imported his rum from Jamaica and his sherry, port, claret, and Madeira from Europe, but probably he was drinking local brandy and local cider.

Cut off from their beer-dependent relatives back home, the new Americans tried a little of everything. (See "Making Your Own," appendix A.) The apple trees planted by the earliest comers flourished, and hard cider became the most popular drink for young and old. It was local and cost around three shillings a barrel, and it was easy to make, simply by pounding the fruit to a mush and letting it sit. The juice was filtered through fresh straw which, after you'd finished squeezing out the cider, made excellent food for pigs. The pigs were said to find it "highly acceptable." Perhaps they were dancing in their sties.

Homemade cider wasn't something you'd serve to dinner guests, but there was always plenty on hand. According to his son, "to the end of John Adams's life a large tankard of hard cider was his morning draught before breakfast." This might be worth trying; in spite of a lifetime of ailments, both real and imaginary, he lived to be well past ninety, not easy to do at the time.

Distilled cider produced applejack, and New Jersey's "Jersey Lightning" was considered the finest. Virginia and Georgia were famous for peach brandy. Doctors prescribed generous tots of whiskey or rum for colds, fevers, frostbite, snakebite, broken legs, melancholy, and nervousness; brandy was the preferred anesthetic; beer was considered the only cure for scurvy, headaches, and sore muscles; brandy punch cured cholera; rum with a splash of milk in it was prescribed for labor pains.

Like Falstaff, everyone believed that the stronger the drink, the stronger it made the body and soul. The sheer feebleness of water, even if it wasn't full of typhoid and E. coli, reduced the drinker to a flaccid, quaking jelly. One life insurance company raised its rates for the nondrinker, who was "thin and watery, and as mentally cranked, in that he repudiated the good creatures of God as found in alcoholic drinks."

Mourners, as in ancient Egypt, cheered the passage to the next world with a supply of rum tucked into the casket, then drank the leftovers. In classrooms all over the colonies the pupils, who had probably had ale or hard cider for breakfast, were entitled to morning and afternoon breaks for another drink or two. If they went on to college they were even more generously rewarded; Harvard had its own brewery and made its own cider, which John Adams remembered as "refreshing and salubrious, hard as it often was."

In the courtroom, bottles were passed around and shared by plaintiff, defendant, lawyers, and jurors. Drink served as legal tender, exchanged for goods and services, and in Boston, by the 1640s, brandy and grain whiskey were doled out to employees as salary, somewhat to the detriment of their work.

Stagecoaches stopped every five miles to "water the horses and brandy the gentlemen."

The early Virginia lawmakers felt that no one should be "ſuffered to drink more than was neceſſary," but quite a lot was indeed neceſſary, ordained by hospitality, social

codes, basic manners, and the need to revive those overcome by heat or cold. Healths must be drunk at christen-
ings, birthdays, and funerals, and toasts proposed on all
civic occasions to the king, the individual members of his
family, the local governing bodies, and everyone present.

Christmas alone lasted three full weeks.

The young George Washington decided to go into politics, ran for the Virginia House of Burgesses, and lost. Re-
alizing the error of his ways, he ran again, this time
investing in 144 gallons of rum, wine, hard cider, strong
punch, and beer, and handing it out to voters. In return, he
reaped more than two votes per gallon and won; the rest is
history.

Later, he was scolded by the virtuous for passing out
rum to his troops in the field, though the local water was
questionable, and it was a long war and the troops needed
a spot of cheer. "The benefits," huffed the general, "aris-
ing from the moderate use of strong Liquor have been ex-
perienced in all Armies and are not to be disputed."
During the awful winter at Valley Forge the troops got
double rations, and no wonder.

When Washington retired and went home, he had his
farm manager, a master distiller from Scotland, set up a
whiskey still to use the extra grain crops instead of leaving
them to rot. It was a great success, selling over ten thousand gallons and bringing in about three hundred thousand dollars in two years. (Later Lincoln, too, tried distilling
but nothing much came of it. His early years were paved
with failed projects. Jefferson had tried planting grapes but
the wine was disappointing.)

In colonial America taverns were often built next to
courthouses, and settling a matter "out of court" meant

that everyone repaired next door to talk it over. Others were built near churches, so that the virtuous could refresh themselves before and after services. In *Colonial Days in Old New York,* Alice Morse Earle tells us that strong drink was essential for most transactions and served at "weddings, funerals, church-openings, deacon ordainings, and house-raisings. No farm hand in haying field, no sailor on a vessel, no workman in a mill, no cobbler, tailor, carpenter, mason, or tinker would work without some strong drink, some treat."

Imported Madeira had been the beverage of choice for nicer folks; in 1745 Benjamin Franklin penned a jolly drinking ditty concluding, "That virtue and safety in wine-bibbing's found / While all that drink water deserve to be drowned." He said, "Wine makes daily living easier, less hurried, with fewer tensions and more tolerance." (During the Constitutional Convention a quiet bodyguard followed him around to haul him out of taverns before he got in trouble.)

The English sent us the Sugar Tax, which somehow included Madeira and came just before the infamous Stamp Act, which was followed by a tax on tea, as in the Boston Tea Party. The colonials dug in their toes and switched from tea and Madeira to New England rum. Respectable or not, it beat paying taxes. It had a good deal more muscle than Madeira, and its effect on colonial tempers gave the Revolution a hearty push.

Indeed, our Revolution was born and raised in taverns. In *The Alcoholic Republic* William Rorabaugh tells us, "Patriots viewed public houses as the nurseries of freedom . . .

seed beds of the Revolution, the places where British tyranny was condemned, militiamen organized, and independence plotted." The spirits of '75 gave birth to the Spirit of '76.

The fifty-five delegates to the Constitutional Convention worked long and hard, and two days before their work was finally done they adjourned to a tavern for some rest, and according to the bill they drank fifty-four bottles of Madeira, sixty bottles of claret, eight of whiskey, twenty-two of port, eight of hard cider, and seven bowls of punch so large that, it was said, ducks could swim around in them. Then they went back to work and finished founding the new republic.

In the brave new country, drinking a lot was seen as an inalienable right of free men. The Whiskey Rebellion of 1794 sprang from an excise tax on whiskey, which was a blow to freedom and a trampling of our liberties, customs, and habits; an insult to our pride and independence.

Presently the heavy drinking inspired a backlash. As always, the worry was over the socioeconomically disadvantaged who, unlike their betters, might behave irresponsibly and neglect their proper work. In our staunchly democratic society, it was still no scandal for the well-bred to get roaring drunk; they could, as people used to say, "handle their liquor." Besides, they could afford it. The lower orders would drink their poor families out of house and home and perhaps, as in Gin Lane, forget the proper respect due to the upper orders. Become an unreliable element in society. Vote for the wrong candidates.

Thomas Jefferson, who had spent time in France and

presided over an impeccable wine cellar, felt wine was the answer: "No nation is drunken where wine is cheap, and none sober where dearness of wine substitutes ardent spirits as its common beverage." This didn't play; probably most of the heavy drinkers had never even tasted a really good, affordable bottle of French wine.

It was argued that with recent improvements in medicine, alcohol as the all-purpose cure was obsolete. It was argued that if we passed laws limiting the number of taverns and closing the extras, the former customers, finding the door of their favorite tappy locked, would shrug, have a glass of water, and get back to work.

The pro-drinks spokesmen held that the tavern was socially useful, a democratic forum where rich farmers and poor ploughmen drank side by side and traded views; taverns bonded the diverse communities together in a shared pleasure.

Their opponents countered that pleasure itself, any pleasure, worked against strict republican virtues and the devotion to hard work. Besides, the Revolution had been sparked in taverns. What if these drinkers now decided to overthrow their newly elected authorities in pursuit of some different dream?

It was a standoff. Taverns have never been easy to stamp out. They remained, and flourished in growing cities, and in the scattered small farming towns they were the sole source of news and easy companionship. As we spread out and settled new territory, far from old neighbors and friends, they were a godsend, fount of new friendship, the light at the end of the long day's tunnel.

They've lost their point in the twenty-first century. The sportier bars now have, in addition to assorted television screens tuned to assorted entertainment, electronic poker machines bolted to the bar in front of each stool so that to fend off conversation the drinker may put a quarter in and pretend to be absorbed in his kings and aces. Human companionship has dropped far down in our priorities and other people only interrupt more exciting options. But how nobly our taverns did serve us for centuries!

Many Merrie Diversions

Oh I have been to Ludlow fair
And left my necktie god knows where,
And carried half-way home or near,
Pints and quarts of Ludlow beer;
Then the world seemed none so bad,
And I myself a sterling lad;
And down in lovely muck I've lain,
Happy till I woke again.

—A. E. HOUSMAN

BACK IN MERRY ENGLAND, after Queen Anne lurched off to her grave, the various Germanic Georges who followed were indistinguishable to American eyes except for the third, whose pigheadedness inspired our Revolution. As drinkers they were steady but phlegmatic, less inspired than the Stuarts, but their subjects kept up the custom.

Upper-class gentlemen, the "three-bottle men," were much admired for their capacity, and the bandaged feet of port-induced gout were displayed as a mark of valor and a fashion statement. Port was a status symbol. It was drunk in the company of your peers, with as much ceremony as our martinis, and the bottles had to be passed clockwise around the table and left unstoppered: when your host put the cork back in, it was bedtime.

Evelyn Waugh, in *Wine in Peace and War,* credits the port of the Senior Common Room for the unique qualities of British university scholarship, and observes that "the heavy port drinker must be prepared to make some sacrifice of personal beauty and agility. Its martyrs are usually well content with the bargain and in consolation it may be remarked that a red nose never lost a friend worth holding . . . Port is not for the very young, the vain and the active. It is the comfort of age and the companion of the scholar and the philosopher."

Dr. Samuel Johnson, however, was in favor of even stronger stuff; drinking mere wine, he said, threatens people with death by dropsy in their long efforts to get drunk. Boswell persuades him to try a glass of claret, but "No, Sir," he said, "claret is the liquor for boys; port, for men; but he who aspires to be a hero must drink brandy. In the first place, the flavour of brandy is most grateful to the palate; and then brandy will do soonest for a man what drinking *can* do for him."

The ladies, if they couldn't put away as much port, rarely said no and often kept a quiet bottle or two squirreled away in their bedchambers. Unlike the women of Gin Lane, sprawled in the public gutters, what a lady of quality drank was none of your business.

England boasted 150 different recipes for punch, all of them living up to its name. Clergymen of all ranks geared up for their sermons with generous tankards of ale. Every area, every town of any pretensions, had its own incomparable brew and sang songs in its praise.

The lower classes greeted the dawn with something called "purl," warm beer with a glass of gin in it, courage to face the working day. For all classes, gentler drinks were upgraded with a goodly dollop of something more muscular.

Country folk drank steadily and for the most part gently year round, from breakfast table to tavern, moving into high gear for the many country fairs, bright spots in the quiet life, meccas for buying, selling, flirting, and beer. After you'd sold your eggs, lambs, piglets, calves or whatever you'd brought, you had some ready cash and a healthy thirst and you didn't need a designated driver. The horse knew the way home.

When the British navy captured Jamaica in 1655 and discovered its national drink, cheap rum replaced brandy as the sailor's friend. The sailor needed a friend. Shipboard life was brutal, crowded, often dangerous, and involved heavy lifting. The navy, pride and joy of the empire, sailed on seas of rum. Admiral Nelson was doped with rum when they sawed off his arm. As shipboard medicine, it was ready at hand to cure most diseases except helpless drunkenness, for which rest was the only cure.

In early days the rum was issued and taken straight, each sailor his half pint a day. Then in 1740 Admiral Vernon, whom you remember from the War of Jenkins' Ear, decreed that it be diluted with water, a mere quarter of a pint in a pint of water, issued twice a day. (It started out at 160 proof, so it wasn't very sissy even diluted.) The admiral was famous for his grosgrain coat and known as "Old Grog," so his weakened drink was called grog. In 1824 the entitlement shrank to once a day, and shrank again to a quarter pint in 1850, but it wasn't until 1970 that all naval rum was stopped, a shocking breach of tradition.

Officers, of course, could and did bring along their own lavish supplies of better stuff, as Patrick O'Brian tells in his Aubrey/Maturin books, and even the lowly tars had ways of supplementing the daily dole. Drinking off-ration came to be known as "tapping the admiral," and rum was often called "Nelson's Blood," because after Trafalgar, Nelson's body was preserved in a cask of rum and various crew members tapped into the cask with straws while sailing home—respectfully, of course. So popular was this fount that by the time they reached port for the funeral, the fallen hero had been sucked bone dry. (Unfortunately a new biography of Nelson says it was brandy, not rum, and nobody drank it. Maybe. Sometimes a myth is more fun than the truth.)

Whatever, as soon as they got their shore leaves, the sailors headed for the local pubs. No amount of general-issue rum could hold a candle to a jolly good public house, symbol of the homeland, its very name implying welcome to all. The visits were brief. Most of their lives were spent at sea, where rum, not bulky, perishable beer, was the staff of life.

On land His Majesty's troops, the boots on the ground of the empire, tended to go native. In Asia this meant arrak, a ferocious drink compounded mostly of palm sap, maybe touched up with rice or molasses or whatever fruits and grains were handy. It's recorded that during the year 1833, in India, the 710 men of the 26th Foot put away 5,320 gallons of arrak, compared to only 209 of brandy, 249 of gin, and a bit more than 500 of beer. No rum is mentioned. Apparently the navy drank it all.

Rum came from Caribbean sugarcane, from the molasses left over after you'd finished making sugar. On his second voyage, in 1493, Columbus stumbled on it, picking up some cuttings on his way past the Canaries and planting them on Hispaniola, today's Haiti and Dominican Republic. It spread. Like our own apples and peaches, it was more fun to drink than to eat, and a document on Barbados 150 years later reports "the chief fuddling they make on this island is Rumbullion, alias Kill Devil—a hot hellish and terrible liquor."

Long ago Marco Polo reported drinking a "very good wine of sugar" in Persia, but rum as we know it is Caribbean, though now the connection is more with cruise ships, lime juice, and pretty paper umbrellas than with the slaves and pirates who once drank their distilled molasses straight up.

Most Americans preferred whiskey. It was easy. It could be made and sold locally, with local corn or barley, and didn't need ships and a port. It expanded out of the neighborhood still and went professional: Jim Beam sold its first barrel of bourbon in 1795.

A moral shadow hovered over rum because of the Triangle Trade. The British navy needed plenty of rum, and rum depended on slave labor to work the cane plantations. New England ships went to West Africa loaded with rum and other essentials, traded their cargoes there for slaves, then sailed the slaves to the West Indian plantations and sold them for sugar and molasses—and money—and carried the molasses home to New England to be made into rum.

Time passed. America spread westward. Those early gold prospectors and cattle rustlers drank whiskey, since there were no ports to bring rum, no apples or peaches for cider or brandy, and who would haul wagon-loads of beer over mountain and desert to John Wayne's favorite saloon? According to the received wisdom, the bewhiskered, scraggy prospectors came down from the mountains in the spring with their pack donkeys and headed straight for the nearest swinging door for a few stiff ones, followed by a poker game and a brawl with flying bottles. (According to my Colorado grandmother, they actually headed first for the general store and bought up the bottled tomato juice and stood outside pouring it into their open mouths, the first vitamins they'd tasted in months.)

The wine-drinking countries, of course, felt, and still feel, their tastes to be far more refined and sophisticated. Who could doubt that wine is more civilized than rum, and a bunch of grapes more elegant than a tub of barley? Wine flowed freely, prized for its wholesomeness, often laced with a little something stronger to improve the effect. Late in the 1800s Pope Leo XIII graciously allowed his portrait to be used on labels and advertising posters telling the world that he had awarded a gold medal "In Recognition of Benefits Received from Vin Mariani." Ads for the popular Mariani called it "For Body and Brain" and claimed that it "Nourishes Fortifies Refreshes."

Indeed it did. It was a sparkling red with the added benefit of a goodly dollop of cocaine. Cocaine with alcohol makes a psychoactive metabolite, cocaethylene, that blocks the dopamine transporter and produces a perfectly delicious state of euphoria, for which His Holiness was suitably grateful. So were the American presidents Grant and McKinley. So was the Russian czar.

So was Queen Victoria, who took it regularly as a tonic.

Victoria wasn't a two-fisted toper like Queens Anne and Elizabeth, but she liked a wee drop and sternly opposed the "pernicious heresy" of pious nondrinkers. She was also much attached to her Scottish retreat and her beloved Highland servant John Brown. No doubt it was Brown, always concerned for her health, who told her that namby-pamby French wines would weaken her constitution; for health, courage, and fortitude she needed the Scottish national drink.

It's reported that Prime Minister Gladstone was "startled" by her new dinner-table tipple: half a tumbler of red wine, preferably claret, and fill it up with Scotch.

I tried it. It's rather a peculiar flavor, but not half as nasty as you'd think.

The March of the Drys

Father, dear Father, come home with me now.
The clock in the steeple strikes one.
You said you were coming straight home from the shop
As soon as your day's work was done.
Our fire has gone out, our house is all dark,
And Mother's been watching since tea,
With poor brother Benny so sick in her arms
And no one to help her but me.

—TEN NIGHTS IN A BAR-ROOM

WHEN WE SPEAK of "pubs" or "taverns," we speak of jolly comradeship. When we call them "bar rooms" or "saloons," though they serve the same beer, they're the heart of darkness, Satan's recruiting station, and graveyard of family values. *Ten Nights in a Bar-Room* was a madly popular 1854 novel, melodramatic play, and early movie in which Father, enslaved by alcohol, neglects his family until his dear little daughter comes to haul him out of the den of iniquity; the bartender bashes her in the head with a glass, she dies, and Father reforms. Everyone wept.

In the middle of the nineteenth century, America was

convulsed by one of its periodic fits of virtue. Anti-drink, or "temperance," legions sprang up all over, spear-headed by fierce women and the formerly easygoing clergy.

The nondrinkers (Drys) were noisy and obstreperous and the drinkers (Wets) cringed and caved in all over. Between 1851 and 1860, Maine, Oregon, Massachusetts, Minnesota, Rhode Island, Vermont, Michigan, Connecticut, Delaware, Indiana, Iowa, Nebraska, New Hampshire, New York, and Pennsylvania declared all alcoholic beverages illegal. The results were about what you'd expect; during that decade American consumption of beer, wine, and whiskey jumped by 63 percent. Then the Civil War came along and gave people something else to worry about and it all faded away for a while.

After we'd dusted ourselves off from the war, though, temperance rebounded. (The name was a bit confusing, since "temperance" means what we now call "moderation," and these folks had zero tolerance.) We even elected Rutherford B. Hayes president, apparently just because he'd been a big wheel in the Sons of Temperance society and much in demand as a speaker against the evils of drink. He is best remembered today for serving water to horrified foreign dignitaries at White House dinners. His wife is remembered as "Lemonade Lucy."

In the 1870s and '80s hordes of women, crying that drink made husbands hit their wives and kick their children, poured out of the woodwork and onto the sidewalks in front of saloons. The Midwest was overrun with them. Maybe they couldn't vote, but they could kneel and pray and sing hymns without ceasing until the customers fled and the owners closed the doors. They sang:

And where are the hands red with slaughter?
Behold them each day as you pass
The places where death and destruction
Are retailed at ten cents a glass.

We have no statistics on how many chaps had actually committed murders and dismemberments with their bare hands and then ordered a beer without washing up, but the point was clear and the din was terrific.

Later the good ladies recruited small children to march right into the taverns and ask, in a quavering treble, "Have you seen my daddy?"

As soon as the groups moved on, praying and singing, to cleanse another town, the saloons reopened and the customers returned.

As the century wound down, the wandering singers were replaced by the much better organized Women's Christian Temperance Union. "Lips that touch liquor," they vowed, "shall never touch mine." They hung out in schools haranguing small children on the joys of water and making them sign the Pledge.

Carry Nation is our most enduring image of the WCTU and Drys in general, storming out of Kansas, bursting into bars, and swinging her hatchet at the bottles, if not the actual customers.

We have no medical proof, but it's possible she didn't have all her marbles. Her mother was convinced that she was the real Queen of England, Queen Victoria having usurped her rightful throne, and strode regally around in flowing purple robes conferring knighthoods on the astonished local farmers.

Carry's only child was psychotic and confined to a lunatic asylum.

Carry herself died in a Kansas hospital of what was described as "nervous trouble."

However, she had the courage of her convictions, and God Himself had appeared to her and told her that her mission in life was to stamp out everything alcoholic in the whole country, so she abandoned her husband and daughter and marched forth to do His bidding. In the beginning she was armed only with a wagonload of bricks, rocks, and chunks of wood. She marched into saloons and threw rocks at the bottles and smashed the furniture with logs. A daunting sight she was, too, nearly six feet tall with a face like a bulldog, and everyone bolted to safety. Then in a hardware store she found her trusty companion, the famous, far more efficient hatchet, and after that there was no stopping her. Once you've thrown a rock, it stays thrown and you need fresh rocks, but the hatchet never left her hand.

She didn't just smash the bottles. When she was finished with a saloon it was rubble, the chairs and tables in splinters and rivers of whiskey pouring out into the streets.

When the saloon keepers managed to rebuild and open again, the grateful regulars rushed back in, accompanied by hordes of tourists anxious to visit the scene of the carnage. Business flourished in her wake, but Carry kept moving on: God wasn't going to be satisfied with Kansas alone. She went to St. Louis, Chicago, Detroit, and Montana, scattering holy destruction all over. Her awed press coverage filled the newspapers.

As long as she stuck to the Midwestern states, she didn't meet much opposition. Apparently people thought of her as a natural disaster, like tornadoes. They may even have thought she had a point. Not content with these victories, though, she went East, to the darkest dens of iniquity in Philadelphia, New York, and Atlantic City.

The East was less impressed. People suggested that what she was doing wasn't so much a righteous crusade as destruction of private property. She was tossed in jail over and over, and proud of it, but never stayed long; perhaps the authorities didn't want her hanging around haranguing them. Her press coverage fell off. Newspapers stopped sending reporters and sent their humor columnists instead. Cartoonists had a lovely time. From the scourge of God, she shrank into a joke. People were laughing, audibly. She was crushed. She'd been ready, even anxious, for battle, but not for ridicule. Fading fast, she died before she saw the glorious dawn of Prohibition.

Her legacy lingered. In the opening years of the twentieth century, more and more virtuous citizens came to believe that drink was un-Christian, though Jesus had never objected to a few firkins of wine, and possibly the root of all evil, especially for the working classes who, as always, couldn't be trusted with the stuff. The Anti-Saloon League rose up in force, shouting.

When men took over the movement, they shifted the emphasis from wife-beating to job performance. Management urged sobriety to boost production and reduce work-related injuries like falling into the sausage-grinder, while labor leaders like Eugene Debs urged sobriety to boost the laborers' savings accounts. The words "character" and "morals" were bandied about, but as in London's

Gin Lane, the driving force was the need for a working class that worked long and carefully, responsibly, cheaply, and soberly.

In 1919, with the distractions of war once more behind us, we gathered together against the evils of drink and the angel of Prohibition fluttered down to rescue the land of the free. The Volstead Act put teeth into the Eighteenth Amendment, sometimes called "The Noble Experiment." (It wasn't a new experiment; in 1914 Russia had outlawed vodka so as to save the potatoes for food. The populace brooded for three whole years before rising up and overthrowing the government.)

Wilson vetoed the act but it passed anyway. The Reverend Billy Sunday rejoiced: "The reign of tears is over. The slums will soon be a memory. We will turn our prisons into factories and our jails into storehouses and corncribs. Men will walk upright now, women will smile, and the children will laugh."

Somehow the slums didn't vanish, but American drinking got a prodigious shot in the arm. Previously sober, law-abiding people felt it was now their civic duty to protest the law by getting as drunk as possible, which was pretty drunk. For the naturally defiant young, as later with marijuana, illegality made drinking irresistible. (Those wanting to outlaw cigarettes might not have noticed this effect.)

Rum made a comeback. Rumrunners ran it in ships from the West Indies, but it wasn't the best stuff and couldn't compete with homemade gin. However, in Cuba the rum was quite delicious and the exotic setting gave it romantic clout. Through the 1920s and early '30s, ferries and cruise lines carried the thirsty to newly flourishing American bars in Havana. Aviation took wing: ten months after Prohibition kicked in, the first scheduled international flights from our shores took off, Key West to Havana. Ernest Hemingway moved down there bag and baggage and once, they say, downed sixteen double daiquiris in his favorite bar, El Floridita, at a single sitting.

The Reverend Sunday and the good folk of the temperance movement had taken it for granted that without legal drinks all the citizens would overnight turn industrious and pious and spend their free time in church.

It didn't work out that way. Indeed, the American public was having quite an alarming amount of fun.

Martinis, Antifreeze, & Other Forbidden Fruit

I like to have a martini—
Two at the very most.
After three I'm under the table,
After four I'm under my host.

—DOROTHY PARKER

UNDER PROHIBITION, MARTINIS came into their own. For most of the twentieth century, the martini was the definitive drink—called simply a "drink"—among those who felt that what you drank was an essential part of your respectability, your background, and your social, professional, and educational standing. The martini was the signature drink of the ruling class and the passport to all corridors of power from politics to poetry, academia to Wall Street.

People weaned on bourbon or rum-and-Coke or Manischewitz came to the big city to seek their fortunes, noticed, blushed, and switched.

Whiskey can be drunk anywhere, even from a flask,

even alone by your campfire in the desert or jungle, but a martini requires ambience. Martinis were drunk in every speakeasy worthy of the name; the bartender was defined by his martinis. In private, after a hard day's work and with no guests expected, you might come home and simply drop a couple of ice cubes into a glass of bootleg Scotch, because making martinis is always a ceremonious matter. A casual martini would be inappropriate, like reciting Keats while watching football. It would be slightly off-key, though not outrageous, for a woman to make one: it was man's work, like grilling meat outdoors but more elegant, the closest a real man might come to ballet.

A martini represents grace under pressure. An arabesque, a liquid pearl. Somebody said it was Fred Astaire in a glass.

The man of the house presided over the cocktail shaker and waited until the assembled guests, or even just his wife, fell silent, eyes upon him. It was always essential to the martini that it be made at the moment, glasses chilled and waiting. As Bernard DeVoto put it in his classic essay in *Harper's* in 1949, "The proper union of gin and vermouth is a great and sudden glory; it is one of the happiest marriages, and one of the shortest-lived."

Long ago a friend invited me over for drinks after work and, being an anxious, compulsive type, had made the martinis before she went to work in the morning and stashed the cocktail shaker in the refrigerator. I don't know what happens to martinis refrigerated over the working day, but I got sick as a dog and had to spend the night on her couch. Thus is the act of mixing sacred: the moment is the only moment.

The maker measures. He explains his recipe, his brand of gin, his stand on stirred-or-shaken, and his proportions.

This ceremony was the central ritual of a now-forgotten custom called "having some friends over for drinks," not to be confused with the cocktail party, which was an elaborate affair involving canapés and people you didn't want to get stuck with face-to-face. Many, if not most, married couples had originally met over drinks at the home of mutual friends, a gentle venue superior to the current anxious and lonely dating rituals, with conversational backup should words fail.

After marriage, in those quieter times, the husband might come home from work and, signaling the end of toil, his wife would stash the dinner in the oven to keep warm and banish the children from underfoot, and he would shake or stir the martinis, and they would sit down together and ask each other how their day had been. Nowadays, after the children have been picked up from day care and driven to soccer practice and the order phoned in for pizza on our way home from the gym, life is much busier and more exciting, and we never need to know how our spouse's day has been, which may be just as well.

The coastal martini was called a "dry" martini. The wet martini lived inland. The severity of the proportions marked your closeness to the centers of sophistication, diminishing as the coastline receded. At the edges of the country, your host defended gin to vermouth as eight to one, ten to one, or simply rinsing the glass with vermouth, dumping it, and pouring in the gin. Some steamed off the label of the Martini & Rossi bottle and passed it over the glass; others kept vermouth in a perfume-spray bottle and gave the gin a quick misting. Winston Churchill poured the gin into a pitcher and then nodded ritually at the bottle of vermouth across the room. Some called their friends and neighbors to find out if they had any vermouth in the house, and if they did, the phone call made close enough contact with the gin at the other end of the line.

The definitive American food-and-drink authority, from 1931 and decades thereafter, was Irma Rombauer of *The Joy of Cooking*. She lived in St. Louis, Missouri. I seem to remember that in her earlier works she advocated a martini as a mix of gin and sweet vermouth, roughly half-and-half. By 1975, hauled ruthlessly into the modern age, she admitted that it was often mixed with one to two jiggers of dry vermouth to six to seven jiggers of gin, but she didn't approve. "A formula we happen to prefer, and which would be more nearly recognizable by Signor Martini who, presumably, invented the world-renowned concoction three-quarters of a century ago—one jigger dry vermouth, one jigger sweet vermouth, six jiggers of gin, and a dash of bitters."

Three to one, in short, with sweet vermouth. I can hear the companions of my youth howling.

"Signor Martini" is open to question too, as is "three-quarters of a century."

The martini seems to have appeared somewhere between 1862 and 1876, made with four parts sweet red vermouth to one part gin, a dash of Boker's bitters, and a maraschino cherry. Later the Boker's was replaced by orange bitters and the proportions went half-and-half. Then it morphed into dry white vermouth, and by 1900 the cherry was replaced by a twist of lemon peel. Nobody knows when the olive burst on the scene, but it was around by the 1920s when Robert Benchley and Dorothy

Parker were knocking them back illegally and Cole Porter, in the 1924 *Greenwich Village Follies,* wrote, "They've learned that the fountain of youth / Is a mixture of gin and vermouth."

There's a town in California called Martinez that tries valiantly to establish itself as the birthplace of the drink. According to their chamber of commerce, during the Gold Rush days of 1849 a miner came to town, on his way back to San Francisco, marched into the best bar and, having struck gold, demanded champagne. The bartender was out of champagne but offered him something even better, a drink presumably of his own invention. He made it with one part dry sauterne to three parts gin, stirred it with ice, and added an olive. The miner was so pleased he went on to San Francisco and spread the word, instructing all the local bartenders, and from there it went forth to the world bearing the name of its birthplace.

The story has not found an audience much beyond the town limits. The generally accepted view is that it arrived in the 1890s and was named after the vermouth-makers Martini and Rossi.

I've been through Martinez, California, on the train and, though I'm sure it's a charming place to live, it just doesn't look like the home of the martini. Too inland. Hard to imagine they'd have even heard of olives or bothered to stir their drinks with ice in 1849. Besides, they didn't have any ice.

For ages, ice came from frozen ponds and lakes, chopped into sheets and harvested and stored in ice-houses, packed in straw or sawdust. George Washington and Thomas Jefferson had ice-houses. In the nineteenth century, New England did a terrific business shipping blocks of ice all over the world. It was used to keep your food from spoiling too fast. It's unlikely that Martinez, California, had any frozen ponds or bothered to import New England ice to squander on gin.

The first ice-making machine was patented in 1851 by a Dr. John Gorrie of Apalachicola, Florida, where they badly need ice. It was considered blasphemous, since only God should be allowed to make ice, but it caught on just the same, at least on this side of the Atlantic. In England iced drinks are still considered mildly blasphemous.

Years ago, on my first visit to London, I was young and poor and subsisted on bread and cheese and a slowly nursed pint of beer a day. On my last day I counted my shillings and pence and realized I had money to get to the airport with enough left over to buy a drink. I marched into my neighborhood pub and ordered a Scotch. The kindly publican poured it, paused, and said, "Say, you Yanks like ice in your drinks, don't you?" He whipped off his apron and dashed out the front door. Moments later he was back with a cup full of very small flakes of ice, which he dumped into my drink. They melted at once, sending up bubbles. And I remembered that two or three doors down was a fishmonger, whose wares lay staring upward from beds of flaked ice. A faint whiff of fish hovered over my drink.

This explains why martinis never attained the iconic status in London that they enjoyed in Manhattan. A warm martini is simply not the same.

During Prohibition, martinis ruled among the privileged. Since all drinks were equally illegal, it made sense to get the maximum punch from each glassful. Why dilly-dally over an illegal pint of beer when the illegal martini was so much more, well, compact?

A gentleman might still drink a whiskey-and-soda, called a "highball," but he was probably a secure gentleman, a gentleman deep in a leather armchair in his own library, with his private stash of impeccable smuggled Scotch in the wall safe behind the Cezanne, now fitted with hinges. His wife might drink a Manhattan, or an Old Fashioned made with Old Overholt, both rather cloying but somehow respectable, or at least more respectable than gin or whiskey, having more ingredients in them.

Given the stuff most people were drinking, adding some extra ingredients helped to get it down. The origins of the word "cocktail" are pretty murky; you can choose your favorite myth. It first appeared in print in 1806, but as a breakfast pick-me-up of any sort of spirits with some water—proportions not mentioned—and sugar and bitters, not the same thing at all.

The town of Elmsford, New York, claims that in 1776 a local bartender named Betsy Flanagan decorated the row of bottles with a bouquet of white rooster tail-feathers, and a drinker asked for one of those "cocktails," and she poured him something the story calls a "mixed drink" and stuck a white feather in it. This seems pretty flimsy. For one thing, how would the word ever have leaked out of Elmsford, New York, to the rest of the world?

My personal favorite version involves an unnamed harbor-side bar in an unnamed American port city where a very large, hollow ceramic rooster sat behind the bar, and at day's end all unfinished drinks were poured into it. The impecunious could order a discounted drink of this stew, drawn from a tap under the rooster's tail.

Or you can make up your own story.

With Prohibition, being drunk in public leaped up like a Roman candle from a gloomy vice of the working class into a gloriously madcap and romantic fling, the opposite of Babbitt on Main Street, opposite of stuffiness, middle-class bourgeoisity, conformity, stodginess, and your parents. Drunk was fun. It was never called the vulgar "drunk" but by merry new nicknames: squiffy, pie-eyed, lubricated, smashed, loaded, ossified, blotto, or three sheets to the wind. It was sophisticated. It was new, it was creative, it cast off the fetters.

In the literary world, drinking to what we now call "excess" was your passport, your literary bona fides; who would read the words of the sober? Not that this was new—the poet Horace had observed, "Since Bacchus enlisted frenzied / poets among his Satyrs and Fauns, the dulcet Muses / have usually smelt of drink first thing in the morning"—but the twentieth century breathed fresh life into the tradition. Following playwright Eugene O'Neill and the sodden Jack London of earlier years (see his *John Barleycorn*), Scott Fitzgerald, Hemingway, Faulkner, Sinclair Lewis, Edmund Wilson, Sherwood Anderson, Thomas Wolfe, Hart Crane, James Agee, Malcolm Lowry, Robert Lowell, and John O'Hara led the way with prodigious feats, generating wonderful publicity, followed closely by the lesser luminaries in the lighter veins, like Benchley and Parker and Cole Porter. Thorne Smith wrote hugely popular books like *Topper* in which the hero, trapped in a boring, ordinary life, is led by a lovely lady into the transcendent joys of drinking, and drinking, and drinking. Dylan Thomas set the final seal of approval, writing glorious poetry and actually dying of drink, every young poet's new goal. For writers long after Repeal, like the scandalous Truman Capote, the bottle became as essential as the typewriter.

Artists too. The eerie glow of the Green Fairy, absinthe, had shed its inspirational light on earlier painters, the wicked temptress leading them unto modern masterpieces. Distilled from wormwood and first marketed as a cure for most diseases, its side effects included hallucinations, blindness, deafness, convulsions, mania, stupor, and death. It was wildly popular and much praised by Byron, Oscar Wilde, Manet, Degas, Modigliani, Picasso, and its arch-hero, Toulouse-Lautrec. It came out at 150 proof, but the kicker was its psychoactive *thujone,* which did odd things to your brain. After several people had run amok and killed their wives and children, absinthe was officially banned, but the romance lingered on.

Nostalgically, our artists made do: Robert Rauschenberg, now in his eighties, boasts of finishing off a quart and a half of Jack Daniel's every day of his life while establishing himself as America's iconic modern painter.

Great art calls for strong drink.

Perhaps great statesmanship does too. The inspiring voice of World War II, its rousing leader Winston Churchill began each day with a whiskey-and-soda for breakfast and was said to have "slurped through the war on a tidal wave of champagne and brandy," handily whipping the teetotaler Adolf Hitler. Then he took to his bed with some bottles of brandy and wrote all those engrossing history books, stopping for many a restorative nip, and won the Nobel Prize in literature. Strong words feast on strong drink.

Prohibition plummeted federal revenues, though many private revenues soared and law enforcement types from the attorneys general to the cop on the beat made a good thing from it on the side. Drunk-driving arrests jumped by more than 80 percent, but few had to drive far for a drink; in New York alone over a hundred thousand speakeasies opened for business. Out in the countryside, the traditional arts of moonshine were handed down by old-timers and stills sprang up in every hollow and wood-lot. (For instructions on starting your own, see appendix B.)

The moonshiners took pride in the power of their product, giving it affectionate names like White Mule. Many customers swore it was better than the commercial stuff. They sang,

Gonna go to yon holler,
Gonna build me a still.
I'll sell you a gallon
For a five-dollar bill.

A few miles up the road from me here in Virginia was a famous still, run by an enterprising lady with three stalwart sons. Under the rules of the game, when a federal revenuer went to smash up a still, he had to take along a sheriff's deputy from the local county. My neighbor's operation was on a patch of land that straddled three counties, and all her equipment was on rollers. When the Fed came huffing up the mountain with a Loudoun County deputy, she and her sons rolled everything over the line into Fauquier County and waited there till it was time to roll it into Clarke in front of the approaching Fauquier deputy.

The record's unclear but it seems likely that after a few rounds of this game the revenuers gave up. Anyway, like many of the best moonshiners, she stayed in business long after Repeal. By all reports, she made a potent and delicious product.

Apartment dwellers stopped bathing and filled their bathtubs with lethal mixtures of grain alcohol, lemons, orange peels, grape juice, juniper berries, and whatever else they could find. Men posed as priests to get their hands on the sacramental wine, exempt on religious grounds. The poor drank hair tonic, pouring it through a loaf of bread to filter out the oils and perfumes. In the privacy of their kitchens, housewives drank the vanilla extract, exempt because the authorities deemed it too disgusting to swallow. The truly desperate could drain the brake fluid out of their cars and filter and drink it, but it wasn't very good for them. Neither was Sterno, a primitive form of charcoal briquette called "Canned Heat," pinkish jelly to burn in the can for heating your dinner. It was made of denatured ethyl and methyl alcohol that could be squeezed through a rag to produce a poisonous libation known as "Squeeze."

Some, having drunk themselves under the table, never got up again. The gin of Gin Lane had been a deadly concoction; the bathtub gin of Prohibition had the same effect. The law insisted that industrial alcohol contain poison, to keep people from drinking it, but people drank it anyway. Creative producers took the basics and added glycerine and oil of juniper and called it gin, or caramel and

creosote and called it whiskey. A bootlegger with a bottle
of genuine whiskey could pour it into four bottles, fill it up
with water, color it with iodine, and then restore the punch
with industrial alcohol or antifreeze. In 1928 authorities in
New York tested the booze they'd captured and impounded and found that almost all of it contained poison
of one kind or another. Some say fifty thousand Americans
were killed, paralyzed, or blinded by Prohibition.

Women had had their own legal drink since 1875, Lydia
E. Pinkham's Vegetable Compound. Billed as "THE GREATEST
REMEDY IN THE WORLD," it was a specific for all women's
physical and mental ills, fevers, hysteria, weakness, schizo-
phrenia, cramps, and fainting fits. It was understood that,
except for tuberculosis, whatever ailed a woman had seeped
out from her uterus, a dark and unnatural organ, and it
would be indelicate for a doctor to treat or even think
about it, but fine for a lady named Lydia. Pinkham's compound was originally 40 proof, later reduced to 30, and the
more you drank, the better you felt. Other female remedies sprang up, some as strong as 50 proof. They were obviously medicine, not drink, and strict members of the
WCTU belted them down with a clear conscience.

In rural areas still, the backyard dump sites of tumble-
down cabins bristle with the ladylike medicine bottles of
long ago.

There's always a market for drink for nondrinkers. Early
in the 1950s Hadacol stormed onto the shelves and sold
millions and millions of bottles for $1.25 apiece. In South-
ern states with local-option dry areas, it flowed like water.
It cured impotence, diabetes, cancer, epilepsy, asthma, gall-
stones, and tuberculosis, and teetotalers swigged it down by
the bucket. It had, perhaps on purpose, a nasty musty, fishy

taste that reassured the virtuous that it was indeed medicinal, since it was by no means fun. It was, however, 24 proof, which may have accounted for its curative powers.

Mothers swore by Gripe Water, smuggled in from Britain, a specific for crying babies with teething or colic problems. It was 8 percent alcohol and, taken in sufficient quantities, comforted mothers and babies alike. (A version of it is now widely available and some swear by it, but the alcohol's gone and others complain that it's no use at all these days.)

Some insisted that real booze, too, was still medicine, just as it had been held since its birth. One physician stoutly insisted to the *New York Times* that "there is nothing more valuable in an emergency" than a stiff drink, and he prescribed it for everything from nerves to pneumonia and always had a good one himself at the end of the day.

A group of doctors, drinkers, and brewers lobbied Congress fiercely to get beer exempted as a medicine and sold at the soda counters of drugstores. Fierce battles ensued. The bootleggers and the temperance ladies protested. Finally it was agreed that a few discreet prescriptions could be issued for wine and whiskey, but not for beer. (Nobody said it aloud, but beer was the drink of those working stiffs most demoralized by drinking.)

In the White House, President Harding couldn't serve wine to visiting heads of state at dinner but upstairs, in the private quarters, he passed out martinis to his cronies, quietly. His cronies were not the water-drinking kind. He also played golf. During Prohibition golf enjoyed a sudden soaring popularity, since the private country clubs allowed drinks, and Harding caused mild amusement at the Chevy Chase Club by whipping a bottle out of his golf bag.

Elsewhere in Washington, Teddy Roosevelt's unsuppressible daughter Alice made good wine, excellent beer, and "a very passable gin from oranges" in the still in her basement. She was famous for her parties and didn't like relying on the caterers.

Testifying before a Senate committee in 1926, New York mayor Fiorello LaGuardia said the law had had rather a reverse effect, causing Americans to drink over a million quarts of liquor a day, with the highest percentage of whiskey drinkers of any nation in the world. He said, "I will concede that the saloon was odious, but now we have delicatessen stores, pool rooms, drug stores, millinery shops, private parlors, and fifty-seven other varieties of speakeasies selling liquor and flourishing." (Not to mention the taxes we weren't raking in, since the profits all went into unregulated pockets.) Some say that for every saloon that was closed, three speakeasies sprang up in its place.

American crime, formerly the casual hobby of disorganized amateurs, took note of the money to be made and went professional. Bootlegging empires consolidated. Turf wars broke out. Al Capone was the most famous man in the country and in one year alone made the equivalent of today's two billion dollars. In New York Dutch Schultz reigned supreme, monarch of various distilleries and speakeasies. The rumrunners who had started out smuggling cheap Caribbean rum found their profit margin slim, so they graduated to Canadian whiskey, French champagne, and English gin for the speakeasies of rich coastal cities. A ship might carry up to two hundred thousand dollars worth of drink in a single run, and that was serious money then.

Law enforcement was best described as rollicking. Those in charge of the search and seizures either accepted a handful of money to turn their backs or sternly impounded the offending product and took it home and drank it themselves. In 1928 in San Francisco an entire jury was tried for having drunk the evidence, without which the defendant went free.

The crime rate doubled, bribery was institutionalized, the prisons were packed to the rafters, and fun was everywhere. The Twenties were famous for fun. Scott and Zelda Fitzgerald got plastered and frolicked in public fountains. Women, long discouraged in traditional taverns, flocked freely to the speakeasies and smoked cigarettes. Skirts got shorter, dances got wilder, and everyone carried a pocket flask and sang silly songs. They sang:

Show me the way to go home.
I'm tired and I want to go to bed.
I had a little drink about an hour ago
And it went right to my head.

They sang:

O I had a little hen and she had a wooden leg,
And every time she cackled she would lay a wooden egg.
She was the best little hen that we had on the farm,
And another little drink wouldn't do us any harm.

In 1933 Franklin Roosevelt was elected and, being fond of a nice martini himself, got the Volstead Act repealed and broke out the cocktail shaker.

Legality didn't slow the newly converted drinkers down. Indeed, many states clung to prohibition simply because illegality had made it so much more exciting, giving an extra twinkle to every swallow. Or perhaps because moonshine and bootlegging were so much more profitable than boring old liquor stores. (Oklahoma, staunchly sober all its statehood life, repealed Repeal almost before the ink was dry. I understand dancing is illegal there, too. A fun-free zone.)

Many insisted that their favorite illegal sources made a more wholesome and tasty drink than the commercial houses. Late in 2005, Maggie Bates of Kentucky died at the age of 101, having toiled all her life since age 17 as moonshiner and bootlegger to, she said, support her family. She lived in a dry county, under the Southern custom of county option, and many were the customers for an enterprising girl. In the 1940s she was convicted and served eighteen months, but the police must have been reluctant and treated her nicely because she was hugely popular in the county and active in local philanthropy. You just pulled around the back of her house and knocked on the door.

In more sophisticated circles drinking had become what's now called a "lifestyle." The ink on Repeal was scarcely dry before William Powell and Myrna Loy appeared as Nick and Nora Charles in the first *Thin Man* movie, supposedly a detective story but actually a celluloid celebration of the joy of drinking.

Nick orders a drink in a bar. He explains to the bartender that every cocktail should shake to its own particular rhythm, and that a dry martini should always be shaken in one-two-three waltz time. The bartender obliges, and Nick tips it down in a swallow. Asta, their wire-haired terrier, drags Nora into the bar in search of his master, and Nora too orders a drink, then asks Nick how many he's already had. He says six, so to catch up she asks the bartender for another five alongside the first—"line them up here."

When next seen she's wearing an ice pack on her aching head and wondering what hit her. The hangover is not meant as punishment; it's a joke, it's part of the innocent merriment of the drinking life. At the Charleses' parties everyone drinks heroically. On Christmas morning, Nick has a hangover, which he nurses with the hair of the dog while shooting the ornaments off the tree with his new gun. When the happy pair wake up in the middle of the night, they decide to have a stiff drink before going back to sleep. When Nick knocks Nora out cold to get her out of the line of fire, he revives her by pouring whiskey down her throat.

The final scene must have looked like paradise to the Depression-era audience: they're headed for California in a luxury suite on the train, with room service, surrounded by jungles of champagne bottles and laughing merrily. Life is good.

Just twenty years later, the merriment has faded. Meet Bond, James Bond, in Ian Fleming's first 007 book, *Casino Royale*. "Just a moment," he says to the bartender, and proceeds to instruct him: "Three measures of Gordon's, one of vodka, half a measure of Kina Lillet. Shake it very well until it's ice-cold, then add a large thin slice of lemon-peel. Got it?"

He's the wave of the future, the drinker not as merry-maker but as expert, authority, specialist. Not for him the usual vermouth that gave the drink its name, but a brand you've never heard of. Not for him the gin that nourished generations of drinkers, but gin mixed with vodka, exotic newcomer. The new gourmet drinker must set himself apart from the crowd with recondite touches based on his professional knowledge. Otherwise you might think he was drinking for fun.

In *Diamonds Are Forever* Bond's host offers him a sherry and he sniffs it and approves of the vintage. His host retorts that sherry doesn't have a "vintage," and Bond explains that he refers, of course, to the year—1851—of the original wine on which the sherry was based. Elsewhere he declares he enjoys drinking sake, but only when it's served at 98.4 degrees.

This is not a man you'd invite to share your six-pack.

James Bond and Nick Charles are both in the same line of work—tracking down evildoers—and both drink what they call dry martinis, shaken and not stirred, but an ocean of attitude lies between them.

The party's over.

As for that shaking versus stirring thing, many people with no more pressing work to do have been researching it. The traditional authorities, or snobs, feel it should be stirred and not shaken, and that it contain gin and not vodka. A shaken martini is colder than a stirred one, since the ice has swished around more. Shaking dissolves air into the mix, also known as the dreaded bruising of the gin our forefathers decried, making the martini taste a bit sharp, and the shaker will more completely dissolve the vermouth, giving the result a less oily feel to the educated palate.

With the vodka martini, shaking is key, since coldness is more important. According to the cognoscenti, a less than frigid vodka martini tastes like lighter fluid. With the traditional gin martini, stirring is best, since it preserves the desirable smoothness, but a message from the *British Medical Journal* suggests that shaking a martini may enhance the antioxidant effects of alcohol and make your martini marginally more health-giving than the stirred kind. If this is your drinking priority, shake.

Basically, though, it's best to remember that a happy spouse or a genial host or an amiable bartender and a friendly bar, and, if possible, merry companions are essential to the martini experience. And that in spite of current trends to add everything from chocolate syrup to raspberry juice to your 'tini, it really ought to have some gin in it.

> *There is something about a martini,*
> *A tingle remarkably pleasant;*
> *A yellow, a mellow martini;*
> *I wish that I had one at present.*
> *There is something about a martini,*
> *Ere the dining and dancing begin,*
> *And to tell you the truth,*
> *It is not the vermouth—*
> *I think that perhaps it's the Gin.*

> —*Ogden Nash*

The Following Day

*Amid the horrors of penitence, regret, remorse, head-ache,
nausea, and all the rest of the damn'd hounds of hell that
beset a poor wretch who has been guilty of the sin of
drunkenness—can you speak peace to a troubled soul?*

—Robert Burns to Robert Ainslie, 1791

We owe our classic modern description to Kingsley
Amis's *Lucky Jim*: "The light did him harm, but not as
much as looking at things did; he resolved, having done it
once, never to move his eyeballs again. A dusty thudding in
his head made the scene before him beat like a pulse. His
mouth had been used as a latrine by some small creature of
the night, and then as its mausoleum. During the night,
too, he'd somehow been on a cross-country run and then
been expertly beaten up by the secret police. He felt bad."

In the first century A.D. the Roman sage Pliny the El-
der recommended two raw owl's eggs, taken neat the next
morning.

For those too debilitated to get their hands on even one
raw owl's egg, there are multitudinous modern hangover
remedies on the market, some chemical, some compounded

of all-natural organic herbs and simples, bark, leaves, and vitamins from the ever-growing cult of "nutriceuticals." None of them help much, or not unless you deeply, seriously believe in them, and maybe not even then: when you feel really dreadful, it's hard to summon the energy for faith.

For the merry Prohibition generation and their children, the hangover had considerable social cachet. You were a wild free spirit; you were popular and got invited to many parties; you had connections and a reliable bootlegger; you were Scott and Zelda, Nick and Nora, and the morning after was your badge of worldly sophistication. You bragged about your aching head and shaking hands.

Generations crawled out of bed and took Alka-Seltzer. This is a combination of aspirin and bicarbonate of soda, with a dash of citric acid to make the bicarb fizz. It comes in tablets, which you drop into a glass of water and stare at, moodily, till they dissolve. The fizz was part of the procedure, and comedy routines featured the sufferer wincing and shuddering at the noise. Fizzing made it seem more, well, proactive than passive aspirin: see how brisk and vigorous this remedy is, see how it rolls up its sleeves to go straight to work on your problems.

It now comes in a separate morning-after version. Actually, the authorities say, it does a pretty good job, but only if you take it before you go to bed, at which time you may not even be able to find the stuff; you may be in someone else's apartment, perhaps entwined with a total stranger, and no idea where the medicine cabinet lurks. You may be in Cleveland with no idea how you got there. Or it may simply not have occurred to you that you're going to need help, since at the moment you never felt better.

Scott and Zelda's day is done. The glamour is gone. We are not bons vivants, we are slobs. The great American health-and-fitness movement brings shame and guilt down on the hangover's already-aching head, which probably doesn't help. You have strayed from the straight and narrow path of moderation and may not even get to the gym this morning. You suffer, and it's all your own fault. You have sinned against the new religion. Official policies agree; no governmental or major pharmaceutical research touches hangovers, because they're a righteous punishment for drinking, just as pregnancy is a righteous punishment for unpremeditated sex. The National Institutes of Health feel that no research should be done on hangovers, since their possibility acts as a deterrent.

Co-infections may occur, based on the effects of your background, religion, upbringing, and what you remember of what you did and said, as in Dorothy Parker's classic story "You Were Perfectly Fine," in which the sufferer confronts his airhead date of the night before and learns he has made her the happiest of women by proposing marriage.

The mechanics are as follows.

The alcohol passes from the stomach to the small intestine, whence it gets absorbed into the bloodstream, ascends to the brain, and soothes our cares and disarms our inhibitions. Then it travels to the liver to be processed into the metabolism, and the leftovers proceed from the kidneys as piss.

The liver does its job in two steps with two enzymes, alcohol dehydrogenase and aldehyde dehydrogenase. That first enzyme converts your martinis into a very toxic substance called acetaldehyde. This makes you feel awful all over.

The second villain is dehydration, an odd effect of drinking too much, but involves those hyperactive kidneys.

The third, to be seriously addressed, is congeners. These are the tasty additives and enhancements that make our drinks different from one another. They're easily identifiable to the naked eye: darker is bad, lighter is good. Brandy is the most lethal, congener-wise, followed by red wine, rum, whiskey, white wine, gin, and vodka. Bourbon will make your head ache roughly twice as fiercely as vodka. A variety of congeners during the evening, such as whiskey followed by red wine followed by brandy, confuses the system's processors and raises hell.

There may be some help on the shelves. The dedicated folks at HangoverReview.com studied fifty-two commercial remedies (their methodology isn't explained, but may have been heroic) and recommend only Sob'r-K. This has been around for quite a while, apparently, comes with a no-questions money-back guarantee, lasts pretty much forever in the medicine cabinet, and costs about eighteen cents a pill. It works by trapping the congeners in the booze, somehow filtering them out before they can hit you, and should be taken before, during, and after the festivities. The authors recommend keeping a bowl of them out on the table for your guests.

Hangover-wise, it's also good to avoid anything with bubbles in it, and that goes for rum-and-Coke as well as champagne. On the other hand, some hold by champagne as a cure.

The oldest and most popular remedy, colloquially

known as the hair of the dog that bit you, is politically in-
correct, at least in America: one sin cannot be expiated by
another. We're encouraged to take B-complex vitamin
pills. (For those who insist on organic vitamins, these can
be found, if you persevere, in a version made of willow
bark, though combing the stores for willow-bark vitamin
B might stress your poor system even more.) We're told to
call in sick and rest in a dark quiet room, easier said than
done in a household of crying babies, squabbling toddlers,
ringing phones, and dogs whining to be walked.

We're told to hydrate, but only with virtuous liquids
like ginger ale, water, or Gatorade. If they make us throw
up, so much the better, a fine housecleaning. Then we may
move on to some Pepto-Bismol or antacid for the stomach
and ibuprofen for the head. A bit to eat, perhaps crackers
and soup or bouillon. Tomato juice with crackers, and
honey for the fructose, or a banana milkshake made with
honey, because the banana calms the stomach, the honey
boosts depleted blood sugar, and milk soothes and rehy-
drates. Plus the possibility that the very thought of banana
milkshakes may induce therapeutic vomiting.

Coffee may annoy our stomach, but it helps those
throbbing blood vessels to contract. And as soon as we're
up to it, exercise, the new national cure-all. If exercise
causes a relapse, repeat previous steps.

Our ancestors had other plans.

Even the most punitive of authorities admit that the
hangover is basically caused by that precipitous drop in
blood alcohol, rather like the downhill swoop on a roller
coaster, but primly they dodge the obvious answer: slow

the swoop. Far down in their pompous treatise on the matter, the National Institutes of Health admit that "the observation that alcohol readministration alleviates the unpleasantness of both AW [alcohol withdrawal] and hangovers suggests that the two experiences share a common process."

"Readministration" seems to mean the hair of the dog, but this is the worst thing we could possibly do. Not that it doesn't work. Of course it works; they just said so. It's just that the curative touch of that morning drink will inspire us to get rip-roaring drunk all over again and probably turn us into certified alcoholics.

I don't know what social circles the NIH travels in, but I myself have never seen any sufferer, after shakily sipping his Bloody Mary, let out a whoop, grab the vodka bottle, and chug it down.

Readministration as a cure has stood the test of time. Samuel Pepys swore by a couple of mugs of sack; Lord Byron by hock and soda. James Boswell, a notable drinker, found himself ailing one morning in the Hebrides and his host persuaded him to drink a good tot of brandy, which worked like a charm.

In old New Orleans the accepted hangover cure for the well-born class of ladies was four parts ethyl alcohol, one part ether, and a few drops of your favorite perfume. Stir, and sniff from time to time, or dip your pretty hanky in it and wave it under your nose.

W. C. Fields recommended a martini made with one part vermouth, four parts gin, and one olive, to be taken around the clock.

According to the Duke of Wellington, King George IV of England, fond of the bottle, dosed himself with opium

"to calm the irritation which the use of spirits engenders."
Even among the non-royal, opium was a standby widely
used for everything from hangovers to tuberculosis, and
the Philadelphia physician Benjamin Rush, America's
most famous doctor, urged problem drinkers to wean
themselves slowly from booze on laudanum, which is
opium with wine. A popular hangover cure called for two
ounces of opium, one of saffron, a dash of cloves and cinnamon, and a pint of wine, though perhaps in an emergency you could skip the cinnamon.

A splash of Angostura bitters in soda water is an old
standby.

In Evelyn Waugh's madcap early books, his Bright
Young Things swore by Black Velvets, or Blackers, champagne and stout mixed half-and-half in a tall glass, but we
may not always have the ingredients within easy reach.
Waugh himself had his own remedy: take a large lump of
sugar, soak in Angostura and roll in cayenne pepper, then
drop into a generous glass and fill with champagne. He rhap-
sodizes: "The excellences of this drink defy description . . .
almost unendurably desirable." Perhaps even reason enough
to induce a hangover on purpose.

Medicinal champagne has many champions. One authority claims that to prevent jet lag on even the longest
journey, drink one bottle before boarding and then, en
route, a quarter bottle every hour, taking no other nourishment.

In America in the olden days, readministration was routine whether you had a hangover or not. Though Patrick
Henry, I hear, much preferred opium, most of our Found-
ers started the day off with a goodly jolt, often instead of
breakfast; a couple of mugs of ale or hard cider was the

standard. Perhaps they would have had hangovers if they hadn't been stopped in their tracks.

These days in America the Bloody Mary takes first place. Flight attendants on airlines serve Bloodies almost without being asked. Bloodies soothe not just the hangover but the conscience, since they're obviously virtuous, all those vitamins. The bar at the St. Regis Hotel in Manhattan credits itself with the introduction, claiming that it hired its inventor from Paris in 1934. Theirs consists of:

    1 ounce vodka
    2 ounces tomato juice
    2 dashes salt
    2 dashes black pepper
    2 dashes cayenne pepper
    3 dashes Worcestershire sauce

    Mix all but the vodka. Pour vodka over ice. Add mix.
    Stir. Do not garnish. [This admonition comes as a relief to those of us who never know what to do with that enormous stalk of celery, since noisily crunching it down and picking the strings out of our teeth seems antisocial, and if we lay it aside, it drips.]

However, the St. Regis recipe sounds like a lot of work to do at home, what with counting all those dashes of stuff. The lazy may simply keep a can or two of the ready-made mix, vodka, and perhaps some horseradish, and dump them into a pitcher in seconds.

Plain tomato juice is recommended even by the authorities, who secretly hope to see us suffer, and so is bouillon. To enhance the curative effects of bouillon, add an ounce and a half of vodka to two ounces of it, and maybe some ground pepper and Worcestershire sauce if we feel up to the effort. Americans call it a Bullshot, the English a Polish Bison.

Some unregenerate souls suggest a goodly glassful of some sweet liqueur like Grand Marnier or Benedictine, to replenish both sugar and alcohol, but they don't pretend it's wholesome; it does nothing for your conscience and besides, you may be fresh out of Grand Marnier.

Honey and milk, though, are obviously righteous, and the classic Hair of the Dog is made with a tablespoonful each of honey and heavy cream and an ounce and a half of Scotch, stirred with ice, then strained and downed. People eager for quick results may skip the honey and cream.

And, traditionally, resolve never to drink again.

"My Name Is David"

But they also have erred through wine, and through strong
drink are out of the way: the priest and the prophet have
erred through strong drink, they are swallowed up of wine,
they are out of the way through strong drink;
they err in vision, they stumble in judgement.
For all the tables are full of vomit and filthiness,
so that there is no place clean.

—Isaiah 28:7–8

Over the course of the twentieth century, many things
formerly considered personal problems or even character
flaws were upgraded to diseases worthy of respect and
professional treatment. Those who ate too much and then,
worried about getting fat, stuck their fingers down their
throats, became bulimics. Medical experts fell over themselves developing a specialty in this fresh-minted disease,
while others concentrated on those who, in order not to
get fat, never ate anything at all, now called anorexics.

And the town drunk became an alcoholic, formerly an
adjective modifying "beverage," upgraded to a noun.

(Dylan Thomas defined an alcoholic as "someone you don't like who drinks as much as you do.")

None of these ailments have much in the way of recorded medical history. Bulimia, once called bingeing and purging, was used long ago not for weight loss but to make room for still more food and drink, as in Rome's indulgent days. In its newly respected guise it was popularized by Princess Diana of England, widely loved and pitied for her affliction. Anorexia in the past was called "wasting away" and attributed to melancholy, virginity, heartbreak, and sometimes saintliness; sea voyages were prescribed.

But who had ever bothered to doctor the drunk? Even his immediate family considered him only a garden-variety nuisance. In many times and places he blended into scenery where the sober stood out as downright peculiar. The only suggested treatment was locking him up drink-less, at home or in jail, until he could stumble out under his own steam.

In 1795 the *Litchfield (CT) Monitor* published this notice from a James Chalmers: Whereas the subscriber, through a pernicious habit of drinking for many years, has greatly hurt himself in purse and person, and rendered himself odious to all his acquaintances; finding there is no possibility of breaking off from said practices, but through impossibility to find the liquor, he therefore earnestly begs and prays, that in future no person will sell him either for money nor in trust, any sort of spirituous liquors, as he will not in future pay for it, but will prosecute anyone for action of damage against the temporal and external interest of the public's humble, serious, sober servant.

Notice that Mr. Chalmers has taken what the authorities agree is the great essential first step: he admits he drinks too much. He is no longer in denial. He even admits he's rendered himself odious to everyone around. There is hope for Mr. Chalmers in his lonely struggle.

Notice also that he's only giving up "spirituous liquors." He speaks of a limited abstinence, an abstinence lite, since nobody in his time could imagine life without copious amounts of ale, beer, wine, and cider; how would he get through the day from breakfast to bed, what would happen to his social, business, civic, and domestic world? Where would he see his friends, how respond when somebody drank his health, what to do at weddings and funerals and birthday parties? But we wish him retroactive luck in his fight against brandy and rum. Bring Mr. Chalmers another mug of ale.

Since then the drinking bar has been lowered and the abstinence bar raised. Formerly, to be considered a drunk you had to be pretty much incapacitated most of the time, embarrass your family, inconvenience the police, and wreck at least two cars or, before cars, houses. Now a couple of extra nips at a family reunion will have everyone urging you to get help. This is called "intervention," and any loved ones who don't badger you to get help are called "enablers" and morally much worse than you are, maybe even solely to blame for your plight and peril and your future in a cardboard box drinking antifreeze.

One of the problems with alcoholism as a medical matter is that there doesn't seem to be any cure. A kind of addictive allergy with genetic overtones, it strikes some 7 or 8 percent of the American public, dragging the patient back for more and more until he's no longer having any fun at all.

On the Internet the worried drinker can find Web sites

selling organic compounds of herbs and barks that adjust
your brain chemistry, supply extra neurotransmitters, and
tinker with your molecules so that you, the hardened
drunk, can go out and hoist a few with your buddies and
stop while still conscious. Naturally the folks who make
the stuff have to keep adjusting the recipe to fit your particular unique brain, so I expect it can run into serious
money. Besides, while you're testing it, you could get into
heavy trouble.

The more formal medical establishment thinks the
only answer is to stay away from the stuff completely and
forever.

Alcoholics Anonymous was founded almost immediately after Repeal by two men, anonymous even in death,
described by the institution as "hopeless drunks" but also
described as a New York stockbroker and an Ohio
surgeon—food for thought for investors in New York and
surgical patients in Ohio. Their idea was that drunks trying to quit needed a secret fellowship, like the Freemasons,
to cheer each other on and lend a hand in time of need; to
replace the golden companionship of the tavern with the
golden companionship of the anti-tavern; to swear alle-
giance to one another, protect identities, bond, and listen
to each other's problems all night long.

Most forced intimate gatherings of strangers are awk-
ward because you have so little in common, but in AA
everyone has the one big thing in common, the single interest, and it serves as a limitless topic. Detailed confes-
sions, however dull and repetitive, must be made and
received. In the process shame is replaced by a gloomy,
drunker-than-thou pride.

An anonymous friend of mine reported a confessor

who had refused to admit that he drank too much until the morning he looked out the bedroom window and saw his small plane on the front lawn. Apparently he'd been too drunk to find the airfield, so he just flew on home. The other meeting-goers were pledged to believe him and to listen politely and nod sympathetically, and the next night he could go to a different meeting on the other side of town and tell his tale again, only this time the small plane would be a medium-range bomber. Seething, back at the first group, people could rehearse their stories about waking up in the Lincoln bedroom wearing only a ten-gallon hat, or only a g-string and pasties.

Everyone knows that AA is based on its famous Twelve-Step Program, and those who haven't been there probably imagine this is packed with hard-nosed and useful instructions about staying off the sauce. It runs as follows:

1. We admitted we were powerless over alcohol—that our lives had become unmanageable.

2. Came to believe that a Power greater than ourselves could restore us to sanity.

3. Made a decision to turn our will and our lives over to the care of God *as we understood him*. [The italics are AA's.]

4. Made a searching and fearless moral inventory of ourselves.

5. Admitted to God, to ourselves, and to another human being the exact nature of our wrongs.

6. Were entirely ready to have God remove all these defects of character.

7. Humbly asked him to remove our shortcomings.

8. Made a list of all persons we had harmed, and became willing to make amends to them all.

9. Made direct amends to such people whenever possible, except when to do so would injure them or others.

10. Continued to take personal inventory and when we were wrong promptly admitted it.

11. Sought through prayer and meditation to improve our conscious contact with God, *as we understood Him,* praying only for knowledge of His will for us and the power to carry that out.

12. Having had a spiritual awakening as the result of these steps, we tried to carry this message to alcoholics, and to practice these principles in all our affairs.

In short, pretty gosh-darned holy. AA makes no bones about this. Their own Bible, the Big Book, says alcoholism is "an illness which only a spiritual experience will conquer." They aren't fussy about which particular God you lean on as long as it's a Higher Power, and one that, in spite of all the other problems It has on Its mind, takes a deep, sorrowful, personal interest in what you're drinking.

That first step is a killer, though; you aren't likely to wander into an AA meeting in the midst of a fraternity party. Some folk are driven to sobriety by relatives, Jesus, alarming experiences, doctors' threats, health problems, or delirium tremens. (The last is a scary alcohol-withdrawal attack joked about in the past as seeing pink elephants, and I watched a friend go through it, and it's distinctly sobering. The friend, without benefit of AA or therapy, never drank again, but as a cure it's pretty drastic and medically chancy.)

Before you're ready for the meetings, you have to dry

out, or detox, for a few days, and then rehabilitate. Those of the lower socioeconomic strata are likely to do this in the drunk tank or the county jail. The fortunate spend a month or several in expensive care.

Rehab centers are a fast-growing industry and a cruise through their Web sites invokes the most exotic pages of the *Times* travel section. Apparently they're pitched at the concerned loved ones of the drunk in question, calming their consciences with visions of an upscale spa. They have soothing names like The Orchard, The Mountainside, The Oasis. The most-used words are "holistic" and "serenity," followed by "spirituality" and "compassion." Some boast of using the Twelve-Step program; others boast of not using it. There are snow-capped mountains, white sands, blue waters, cloudless skies, pine forests and palm groves, so friends and family can plainly see it's a long tough walk to the nearest liquor store. There's tennis, fishing, beach volleyball. Yoga. Saunas. Chef-prepared cuisine. Meditation rooms. Trance therapy. Even an American Indian sweat lodge.

Uncle Jake's loved ones, desperate to off-load him without a pang of guilt, dig deeply into their pockets.

When he comes out, he may take up nightly AA meetings as a permanent way of life, which is almost as disruptive as binge drinking, or he may give you the slip and beetle into the nearest bar and order a row of doubles, in which case you don't get your money back. But there's another Orchard waiting, another Oasis, and chances are fair that if his liver doesn't give out first, or he doesn't freeze to death on the sidewalk, he will eventually quit, perhaps in sheer exasperation.

He doesn't drink anymore. Alcoholics Anonymous assures him he's not recovered, merely recovering, or what's rudely known as a dry drunk. His brain may not work as well as he thinks it does. Those cells have taken a pounding and their functioning creaks a bit; they may drift around mistily or seize on dubious ideas and pigheadedly refuse to let go. He's likely just fine on ordinary days, following an ordinary routine doing familiar things, but when strange new emergencies strike he may panic, or freeze and simply sit there staring straight ahead while Rome burns.

But at least he doesn't drink. He tells everyone he never felt better. He ignores any hollowness at his heart. In *Love with Daylight,* Wilfrid Sheed has quit drinking and mourns over his past merrymaking, his trips through France with jolly friends, wine tastings, parties in dear little hotels. Not drinking "cost me nothing less than the best minutes of the day and the best years of my life. Or so it seemed at the time. Giving up booze felt at first like nothing so much as sitting in a great art gallery and watching the paintings being removed one by one until there was nothing left up there but bare white walls."

Bare walls, and the morose satisfaction of having conquered your demons. You, designated driver, victorious, morally superior to those less resolute.

Then, as the century dwindled down to its last years, even that pleasure was dragged away. You looked around and lo, all your friends had quit too, and didn't need you to drive them home from the gym.

America Repents

The demon gave a drunken shriek,
And crept away in stealthiness,
And lo, instead, a person sleek
Who seemed to burst with healthiness.

—W. S. GILBERT

AFTER MANY A MERRY CENTURY, at the end of the twentieth a great wave of Puritanism swept over America. Prohibition struck again, this time self-inflicted. Americans had spent the past two decades in rowdy indulgence, some of it illegal and hallucinatory, and they did repent themselves.

In the 1960s and '70s a foreign substance had crept in and corrupted our youth. Called marijuana, or cannabis, or pot, or weed, it was not drunk but inhaled, and it was alien to all our traditions. It had started among jazz musicians, a dangerous crowd, and wafted out over the land until being stoned became far more stylish than drinking, and all the more so since drink was now legal and the new stuff wasn't.

The authorities, who were older and had never tried it, ran in circles, terrified. Scholars looked it up and found that Very Early Man had probably nibbled on it and found it good in Asia and the Near East, and that the ancient Assyrians, Scythians, Israelites, Chinese Taoists, and other foreigners had probably burned it as incense, leaned over the smoking censers, inhaled, and enjoyed. It may have inspired exotic, unorthodox religions with its euphoria and hallucinations.

It was the foreignness that frightened folks: we didn't inherit this; our grandfathers didn't smoke this. Pot had no connection with good old European beer or whiskey; its effects were different. Instead of reconciling us to the world—"For malt does more than Milton can / To justify God's ways to man"—it seemed to offer glimpses of quite a different world. Instead of singing rude songs, its beneficiaries retreated into an inner space where they couldn't be reached, even by telephone. It had leaked out of alien cultures and wormed its way into America's innocence by way of unhallowed places like New Orleans and New York, poisoning even our wholesome heartlands.

It distracted our young from their studies. They let their hair grow long and wore nontraditional clothes. They criticized the government. They became strangers to their parents, even disrespectful, and bizarre smells crept from under the doors of their bedrooms. Morally, mentally, socially, and patriotically it was far more dangerous than our ancestral drinks and promoted a relaxed attitude, called laid-back, that threatened the whole industrial-economic structure.

The authorities called it a "gateway" drug, meaning that those of our youth who smoked reefers would, by Tuesday, progress to heroin and collapse in alleys poking themselves with needles. Horrendous jail sentences were imposed for pot crumbs in a child's pocket, and for a while there, every child's pocket had pot crumbs.

Then it went away. Its disappearance didn't seem to have much to do with the jail sentences, or the police patrolling the schools. It just left, and most of its young fans cut their hair, went back to school and got their MBAs and took up a serious interest in money, becoming perhaps the stuffiest generation since Victoria.

The backlash was epic. An obsession with one's personal health and longevity swept over the land and replaced all former moral and civic virtues. Wellness and godliness were one and the same. Self-denial was the new self-indulgence. Perfectly healthy people thought about their health morning, noon, and night and exercised till they fell exhausted. The president himself said that fitness was the number-one attribute that Americans needed, wanted, and expected in their president.

Some people ate nothing but broccoli, some ate nothing but lentils, and everyone quit smoking and forswore all forms of what they called "alcohol." Drinking anything but water, coffee, and Gatorade was called "abusing alcohol," as if drink were the victim, though alcohol seems to have survived millennia of abuse and keeps coming back for more.

Hold-outs who ate hamburgers and sat on bar stools and declined to jog spread a miasma of moral gangrene around them that was dangerous to decent folk; those who lit cigarettes on the sidewalk spread cancer for blocks around. Believers neglected their families, not in taverns but in gyms, working out on treadmills for the greater glory of the new gods. Everywhere they went they carried small plastic bottles of water to display their salvation, as one might formerly have worn a hair shirt and carried a cross. Discarded plastic water bottles litter our roads, choke our beaches and rivers, and overwhelm our landfills.

It would be pleasant to suppose that at least some of the brisk businesspersons on the morning sidewalk, briefcase in one hand, bottle in the other, had poured out the water and replaced it with vodka, but I doubt it. They believe.

In the publishing and advertising worlds, the lunches of editors, agents, clients, account executives, and writers, formerly world-famous for martinis, are now companioned by jeroboams of water, iced in the silvery long-legged chalices once used for champagne. Legislators have water lunches with lobbyists. Wellness succeeded where the Volstead Act failed.

Mark Twain observed that "Water, taken in moderation, cannot hurt anybody," but he certainly didn't mean it should replace a genuine drink. No major civilization ever arose from a land of water drinkers. No warm, cooperative sense of community ever sprang from neighbors sitting down together to drink water. As for culture, two thousand years ago the poet Horace said (in Latin), "No verse can give pleasure for long, nor last, that is written by water-drinkers."

In the past and still today in many places, water has been the most dangerous of drinks. The reason so many miracles happened at springs and so many towns have been named for springs is that water that didn't kill you was a discovery to celebrate.

Even paying cash for it doesn't guarantee anything. When director John Huston insisted on filming his masterpiece *The African Queen* in the deepest outback of the Congo, the whole crew loaded up with commercial bottled water, purchased at great expense. Katharine Hepburn's father was a urologist, and she was brought up to believe in drinking water and lots of it. Whatever was in it, the whole crew got sick, but Hepburn was sickest of all, having drunk the most, and had to be airlifted to London for treatment. She lost twenty pounds.

Only Huston and Humphrey Bogart escaped, having stuck to whiskey, and sat around having a few stiff ones and waiting for the rest of the crew to recover from the water.

Europeans, finding water bubbling up on their property, bottled and labeled it and set forth to sell it. Their advertising campaigns were almost religiously inspiring, and while they didn't quite promise miracles on the order of Lourdes, the effect was similar. They spoke of health-giving minerals, and clean blue skies, and purity, and prehistoric sources deep beneath the rocks. Hypnotized, Americans scorned their own and drank oceans of imported water.

Perrier first washed up on our shores in the late '70s, just in time for the tide of reform, and, being French, had a wine-like glamour without the evil of alcohol. In 2004 Americans drank twenty-four gallons of bottled water each, spending nearly $10 billion on the spindly stuff and pitching thirty million plastic bottles a day in the landfills. Roughly 70 percent of their contents had been drawn from municipal taps, the same stuff that runs into your bathtub, which is just as well, since city water is ruled by stiffer regulations than the fancy kind and constantly tested, but bottled and labeled and price-tagged it definitely makes us feel more important than just filling a glass at the kitchen sink for free.

As the competition heated up, water branched out and enhanced itself into cocktails of vitamins, stimulants, caffeine, cucumbers, and promises of strength and health.

Of course water, good water, has always been important. Beer being 90 percent water, in beer countries water has always been sacred; connoisseurs discussed how the beer made from the water hereabouts is mellower, and from over in the next county, sprightlier. Water was an essential ingredient. In the past, though, few people drank it straight unless they were lost in the Sahara.

The virtuous supplement it with coffee. The cognoscenti discuss coffee as if it were wine, and claim to be able to distinguish at a sip between the Ethiopian and the Colombian bean, perhaps even pinpoint the very plantation on which it was grown.

Caffeine is less soothing than alcohol. After coffee came to Europe in the sixteenth century, anxious rulers sent spies to eavesdrop in coffeehouses on the mutterings of the discontented, not to listen in taverns to the toasts and songs of the happy.

In coffee-drinking nations, people align themselves with their extended families and tribes, not with friends and neighbors. They identify with the cousins who come to the house for coffee, not with the fellow customers at the tavern. Caffeine does not encourage relations with strangers; it inspires the alert suspicion essential to self-preservation. Far from softening the harsh edges of reality, caffeine sharpens them, and rouses the exhausted to fresh efforts and longer hours of toil.

To have a drink with someone implies a cozier bond than having coffee with him; a negotiation made over drinks implies a happier outcome than the deal struck over coffees.

Though most dedicated coffee drinkers own fancy machinery for grinding and brewing the stuff, they drink it mostly in specialty coffeehouses, where the stiff prices are part of the mystique; no longer can the classic bum beg a dime for a cup of coffee. The huge, inescapable chain now taking over the landscapes of the world offers enhanced and flavored concoctions so arcane that only the hard-core customer knows what he's ordered. He considers these places the new, healthful, socially approved taverns, but they're not. No resemblance. Most of the customers, being busy and important, carry their cinnamon dolce lattes or whatever out the door to drink them alone. If they stay to sit down, an unwritten law declares that they mustn't speak, or even nod, to strangers. To remind us that, though sitting, they too are busy and important, they whip out their laptops and cell phones and work. Nobody smiles. Odd to think that in the seventeenth century coffeehouses were considered hotbeds of plots and insurgencies and uprisings. Now tactful, noncommittal silence reigns.

Desperate to join the coffee movement, America's largest brewery, Anheuser-Busch, in 2005 put out a caffeinated beer. A ten-ounce can is loaded with the jolt of half a cup of strong black coffee. Too much, and the drinker is not just incoherent but wide-awake and excitable. Another newcomer, called Sparks, is billed as an "energy-drink beer" and contains alcohol, caffeine, ginseng, and guarana. *Rolling Stone* reviewed it, saying, "The wave of the future is getting invigorated and wasted in one go." However, they add that it tastes like cough syrup.

Actually, Frederick the Great of Prussia, in the eighteenth century, pioneered the concept. He always drank seven or eight cups of coffee for breakfast, but he brewed it with champagne instead of water.

Coffee aficionados in America, anxious for something more to worry about, worried about caffeine, and many took to caffeine-free, all-natural herbal teas, carrying a selection of the bags around at all times, each flavor promising to fortify a different aspect of one's constitution, and asked the waitress only for a cup of hot Perrier.

As the twenty-first century loomed, the dairy industry produced an enormous advertising campaign telling us that milk, cow's milk, was the road to health, fitness, and immortality, though nobody explained why humans, alone among the mammals of the world, should drink the stuff after infancy. Maybe, because innocent infants do drink it, it wears a halo of innocence, a virginity restored, or a promise of life everlasting.

Some fifty years earlier in France, Premier Mendès-France recommended milk to the French and actually drank it in public, causing outrage; it was called "a slap in the face to all Frenchmen," and he and his cabinet were voted out of office.

In America beautiful celebrities were hired to appear in ads with a white moustache of what might have been toothpaste under their noses, praising milk. Somehow, though, milk drinking proved no more socializing than water drinking and never became a compelling reason to invite your neighbors over, nor to meet up in milkeries on the way home from work. The story never really took root like water or caffeine, and carrying a bottle of milk simply didn't improve your status like carrying Pellegrino.

The other problem was fat, because fat had turned evil and gave us heart attacks and was an inevitable component of milk, so the virtuous shopped the shelves for milk with less and less of it, until it grew pale gray and tasteless, but ever more virtuous. Every dairy product was now available with pretty much no dairy left in it, all the more morally pure.

There are no good milk-drinking songs. No weary traveler of old was ever welcomed in out of the storm to sit by the fire with a glass of milk, neither do many toast their friends in Pellegrino. As of this writing our president, a strict teetotaler, visits foreign heads of state and, with his place setting crowded by wine glasses ready to receive the noblest vintages his host has to offer, calls sturdily for the diet soda his aides have brought along. At celebrations and anniversaries, the assembled company rarely has too many herbal teas and pounds the table and belts out, "For he's a jolly good fellow, which nobody can deny!" Few winning baseball teams douse their teammates with decaffeinated coffee. Social life has quieted down considerably.

No longer allowed to drink or smoke, Americans had nothing left to do but eat and get fatter and fatter. By 2004 the United States had plunged to a miserable twenty-sixth, far down on the civilization scale, among forty-five countries surveyed for their drinking capacity. The top ten, in descending order, are Luxembourg, Hungary, Czech Republic, Ireland, Germany, France, Portugal, Spain, Great Britain, and Denmark. Not too shabby a gathering.

Currently, over in England, the traditionalist beer

drinkers and the moral authorities join in condemning, to no avail, the craze for alcopops. Originally an alcoholic lemonade, the idea was an instant hit and quickly blossomed into over a hundred brands, including low-calorie diet versions, orange, cranberry, vanilla, tangerine, and dandelion. Sweet and colorful, they're packaged with cartoon characters in bright colors to appeal to the young. The very young, too young to have developed the acquired taste for beer or whiskey but old enough to enjoy a buzz.

British protests seem to be more about traditional culture than underage health, but they're having a spot of trouble with tradition too. Groups known as "lager louts" drink too much beer and wax unruly over sporting events and are clearly not out of the top drawer, being beer drinkers; nobody complains about "Merlot madmen" or "martini maniacs." The problem, however, has to do with the neighbors complaining, not with the health of the loutly.

In America the health guardians lurk and spring. Recently in a restaurant near Seattle, a pregnant woman ordered a pink daiquiri with her lunch. Two waiters furiously refused to serve her and lectured her at length about the damage she would do her unborn child, likely to be born with two or more heads if she drank a daiquiri. She complained to the manager, who managed to get her a drink, but the waiters still scowled and shook their fists.

The police joined the movement. As the twenty-first century dawned, Americans began to obsess about the

problem of Driving While Intoxicated, or Under the Influence, which, according to its loudest opponents, killed
more people than the Black Plague ever did. Laws and
limits were enormously popular politically. The national
standard for drunk driving was set at .08 percent of alcohol in the blood, but local authorities could set their own
limits.

Last spring a nice lady in Washington, DC, went to a
dinner party and, during the meal, drank a glass of red
wine. Driving home down the brightly lit streets of the
city, she forgot to turn on her headlights and was pulled
over by the police. They tested her for alcohol and found
her at .03, handcuffed her and hauled her off to the
hoosegow for DUI. As they proudly explained, the Washington police can arrest anyone driving with a blood-
alcohol level of over .01 percent, or about a third of a glass
of wine with dinner. "Zero tolerance," it's called. Most
first-time offenders can avoid jail time by agreeing to
counseling sessions for their alcoholic sins.

Washington was once a party town; everyone knew that
all the important deals, trade-offs, contacts, legislative
agreements, journalism, leaks, lobbying, and useful friend-
ships took place after office hours, at the lobby bar of the
Willard or the amiable homes of the great Georgetown
hostesses, who took their roles seriously. Most guests drank
more than a third of a glass of wine.

Those who live in the city take taxis anyway; the very
rich can keep their chauffeurs nodding off till the party's
over; but now most folks have moved to the far suburbs
with no way home but the car.

The once well-oiled wheels of the Capitol creep down

to a stop and the lights go out. The last federal consensus withers as Democrats and Republicans rub shoulders no more. Useful contacts are made only at scheduled prayer breakfasts or Texas quail hunts, and future political allegiances will be cemented by cell phone. The lobby at the Willard, which gave birth to the verb "to lobby," looks back in silence.

Experts and
Fashionistas

But Noah he sinned, and we have sinned; on tipsy feet we trod,
  Till a great big, black teetotaler was sent to us for a rod,
And you can't get wine at a P.S.A., or chapel, or Eisteddfod.
      For the Curse of Water has come again because
        of the wrath of God,
      And water is on the Bishop's board and the
        Higher Thinker's shrine,
    But I don't care where the water goes if it doesn't
        get into the wine.

—G. K. CHESTERTON

As soon as all right-thinking people had switched to bottled water, embarrassed mutterings from the medical world were heard in the wings. It seems that the Europeans who were selling us their water and spending the proceeds on wine were actually healthier than we were. Happier. They lived longer. They had fewer heart attacks and strokes. Lower blood pressure and cholesterol. Research exposed the alarming news that red wine deserved the credit and also contained something called trans-Resveratrol, useful against cancer.

The chemists tried hard but found no way to separate the health part from the merriment part: grape juice wouldn't do it. Maybe, after all, we should hold our nose and take a swallow. Tentatively the authorities suggested as much as two glasses of red wine a week, as long as we weren't pregnant, or likely to get pregnant, or taking any other medications. Or elderly.

Then the news got worse. Diabetics who drank had a 79 percent lower chance of dying from heart attacks; all drinkers had a 90 percent lower chance of getting hepatitis from eating raw oysters; drinking helped prevent cataracts and macular degeneration. Older women drinkers were less likely to break their hips. The Finns found out that a bottle of beer a day reduced the risk of kidney stones by 40 percent.

At the University of Wisconsin a study showed that dogs of all breeds improved the length and quality of their lives and reduced the risk of blood clots by drinking beer, the darker the better; Guinness Extra Stout was the best, Bud Light not worth the effort.

In the fall of 2004 the University of Texas at Austin produced a study of older women, average age seventy-five. The results showed that those who knocked back at least a daily splash of anything alcoholic, even whiskey, were sharper and merrier than their abstinent counterparts, with less depression, more energy, better memories, and a jollier outlook. Then, the following year, a long-term study of twelve thousand women age seventy to eighty-one was released by Brigham and Women's Hospital in Boston. No doubt about it, in addition to the already touted heart benefits, the drinkers had crisper memories and firmer thought processes than the abstainers. The conclusion suggested at least one drink a day for the ladies and maybe two for men.

An Irish nursing home recently installed a bar on the premises so that the inmates—average age eighty-five—will feel better and live longer after a nip or two, and besides, their loved ones will come more often to hang out and visit.

And now a new study shows that people who dutifully swallow the mandated eight full glasses of water a day are diluting their blood and in danger of potassium deficiency and early Alzheimer's.

All right, all right, since our health is the only thing that really matters, perhaps we should occasionally have a drink or two, though not, of course, for fun. Always medicinally and always in moderation. The word "moderation" is repeated over and over, as if without this warning we might let out a whoop and greet the dawn with brandy like our Founding Fathers; we might be late for work, or leave the office early for happy hour. Martyrs to moderation, the formerly two-fisted Texans took to drinking Lone Star Specials, a mixture of Merlot and 7-Up.

Moderation is a fairly relative term. In the seventeenth century the British, trying to impose moderation on their citizens shouldering the white man's burden in India, set the ration in their communal dining halls at only a quart of wine and half a pint of brandy per man per meal (it's unclear whether this included breakfast, but I suspect it did). By the beginning of the nineteenth century the rules tightened, admitting just four bottles of wine per day per gentleman, though only one per servant, since the servants needed their wits about them to get the gentlemen to bed, and the wine they were drinking was powerful stuff by modern standards.

Currently in America, the sterner holdouts still feel that two glasses of wine per week should be enough for the health benefit: remember, it's medicine. Do Not Exceed Recommended Dosage.

We have aspirin now for toothache, Prozac for comfort, Valium for courage, Ambien for a night's sleep, and professional counseling for life's hard knocks; why drink except for cardiovascular health?

Well, maybe to show off. After medicinal benefits freed the broccoli eaters from total abstinence, stylish cliques turned drinking-in-moderation into a high-class avocation. They stopped arguing about their brands of spring water and went on wine tours of foreign lands. The rich and famous abandoned their yachts and invested in vineyards instead, and put their portraits on the labels and gave boring interviews about the pedigrees of their grapes. They argued with each other publicly about the superiority of the delicate Pinot over the hardier Merlot (though really nice women still drank only white wine; like the white meat of chicken, it's less nourishing but so much more ladylike). At wine tastings the elite merely rinsed their mouths with the stuff, rolling their eyes thoughtfully, took notes, and spat, clear proof that they had no baser motives.

Not to be outdone, formerly unsophisticated beer drinkers joined in. They scorn mass production and take a serious interest in microbreweries; they sit in brew pubs, where they drink discerningly while gazing upon the very vats and pipes that are even now, or so the bartender says, cooking up their next round.

Former beer joints gone classy offer beer tastings in little sample glasses for the educated palate. Recently a new breed of ale has sprung up, to respectful notice, so elegantly brewed, so complex and nuanced, that it can't be called ale at all, it's "barley wine." Its customers are quite, quite different from sweaty old Joe Six-Pack with his canned Budweiser. They're discriminating experts of an entirely different social class with an entirely different agenda.

Of course drinking, old-fashioned drinking, is still unwholesome, still bad for the body if not the actual soul, but fortunately, what they're doing isn't drinking at all. They aren't drinkers. They're connoisseurs and critics, priests of ritual, sniffers and tasters, discerning scholars scowling thoughtfully into their glass. Fun has nothing to do with it and they never break into song. The waitperson who brings their wine list is always male, formally dressed, unsmiling, and many social rungs above that frilly cocktail waitress who used to bring a martini.

Everyone upgrades. Bourbon competitions are held and gold medals awarded. Recently plain rum has picked up a veneer of respectability and acquired a cult following of aficionados who compare the newest brands and write reams about their nose, their oak overtones, their butterscotch aftertaste. Respectable people can now go into a bar and order a glass of rum and nobody will stare, though others among us would miss the lime juice and the paper umbrellas and the marimbas in the background. Even a few unregenerate whiskey drinkers discuss comparative single-malts and go on Scottish tours and learn about the charring of oak barrels. An even smaller splinter group has started making mead and drinking it in Renaissance costumes.

No longer for pleasure and fellowship, no longer to soothe the wounded spirit or the broken heart, no longer for merry gatherings and rowdy songs, niche drinking has become a cultural hobby, like baroque harp music. You would never admit for a moment that after a second bottle of that modest but irreproachable little vintage, you were feeling no pain. You are a knowledgeable specialist, selecting and appraising your glassful and critiquing every swallow.

It's solitary work, though, and does little to patch up the social web that unraveled in the '90s. A recent survey finds that one-quarter of all Americans have nobody at all to talk to, while the rest mostly confide only in their spouses. When the spouses leave or die, they sit by themselves.

Seeking advice and comfort, we buy a book about our problems or pay a therapist to listen the way our buddies and the bartender used to listen. On campuses all over the country, the young who once argued philosophy around pitchers of beer are playing video games alone in their rooms. After work in the cities, the former denizens of happy hour watch television while they pump the treadmill, silently. Or, dressed in skin-tight Spandex, they tie up traffic on the local roads on bicycles, staring straight ahead as if out-pedaling death itself, and they are, they are; the newest report from the Cooper Institute of Aerobic Research proves that if we spend most of our lives in violent, lonely exercise, we could live to be 120, though it doesn't say why we would want to. Nor why, in the long-ago past, our serf and peasant and slave ancestors who exercised mightily in the fields were dead at 30, while their soft-handed, plump-bellied bosses lived on and on.

Alone, we swim laps.

The detachment is spreading. In France the once-essential bistros are closing down all over and their owners complain that nobody comes to talk anymore, and stricter drunk-driving laws and the threat of a smoking ban keep the customers at home, connected only electronically. The pubs of Old England are smoke free but declining.

In America, in the metropolitan haunts of the highly sophisticated, the cocktail is no longer an instrument of friendship but a competitive fashion statement, or one-upmanship.

A writer for the *New York Times,* whose happy assignment is to keep tabs on who's drinking what and where, cruises the better sort of places and takes note of the new delights they invent and tries to worm out the recipes, though the bartender who came up with the Great Pumpkin Martini refused to give the secret of hers, which the reporter calls "squash on the rocks."

On a recent visit to a revolving watering hole over Times Square, catering to the out-of-towner, he checked out the drinks around him. It seems the Cosmopolitan, for a while the mark of true New-Yorkerhood, has already fallen from local favor and our reporter sees only one, and that's in front of a woman from Mexico City, which is a long way out of town. (For the rubes among us, a Cosmopolitan is, or was, created from lemon- or ginger-flavored vodka, Cointreau or Triple Sec, raspberry juice, and lime juice.)

Last winter's martini of choice was called a "dirty martini," and this actually has a history. Credible sources say that at the Tehran Conference, late in 1943, Franklin Delano Roosevelt brought along his supplies and made Stalin a drink consisting of two parts gin, one part vermouth, and olive juice. Stalin didn't like it. We do not know whether this was Roosevelt's usual recipe or perhaps a cruel joke. Given his elite East Coast background, it seems unlikely he always made them two to one. (It's even less likely that Churchill joined them, his recipe was pretty strict.)

The *Times* reporter also spots a ginger martini and a chocolate martini, the latter being consumed by a New Yorker, no doubt presaging a trend. As a New York bartender recently decreed, "If you serve it in a martini glass, it's a martini." The glass is what people like, the iconic glass, seductive and angular as a Modigliani drawing. Its sharp-cut triangle still sparkles with sophistication, with edge, with New-Yorkness, even in Cleveland, even when it's full of chocolate syrup and raspberries.

What, on his expense account, does our reporter order? This time, the popular Floradora, though in former days most men would have died of thirst rather than ask out loud for such a thing. You put an ounce and a half of raspberry-flavored vodka, half an ounce of lime juice, and an ounce of raspberry syrup in a glass of ice. Fill with ginger ale and add a lime slice and an "edible flower," exact type unspecified, though you wouldn't want anything vulgar like a geranium. "Edible" is specified, so I assume you're expected to sit there at the mahogany bar on your chrome-and-leather stool, looking bored and sophisticated and eating a daffodil, with pollen on your chin.

Also in former days, a grown man ordering a drink with a flower in it, even if he didn't eat it, would have been driven from the saloon with catcalls and violence.

One Floradora is a status symbol, two might induce vomiting, and a raspberry-flavored hangover doesn't bear thinking about.

Then spring came and all the drinks had to have a colorful springtime look, preferably orange, with a slice of mango, and the martinis were made with pomegranate juice or watermelon schnapps. Green apple was out, blackberries were in. Lime leaves will soon replace kumquats. Hibiscus was the new decoration, though no one says whether you have to eat it.

By summer, blueberry vodka was edging out the raspberries.

Cocktails, like women's fashions, must change with the seasons, and the bartender must stay ahead of the pack with new inventions; how else to get written up in the *Times*? Not for pouring a dramatic Scotch on the rocks. It's important to serve and to order today's drink or, better, tomorrow's.

Price counts too. Not only are you up-to-the-minute, you're also very, very rich or, if you're a bar, very expensive. Word just in from Chicago on the lifestyles of the young and carefree: nice young couple on a first date starts with a bottle of Dom Perignon at $350, drinks it, and for chasers orders the cocktail called the Reserve Ruby Red. Made with super-premium Grey Goose L'Orange vodka, Hypnotiq liqueur, orange and pomegranate juices, and a topping of more Dom Perignon, it's stirred by a swizzle stick with a one-carat ruby attached. Not served in a pitcher, as you might expect from the price, but in a martini glass. For $950. Apiece. Perhaps few customers, even in the flush of a birthday, promotion, or new romance, offer to buy a round for the bar.

New York, not to be outdone, offers the Duvet Passion, a cocktail of cognac and champagne garnished with an orchid petal for $1,500. Mindful of its big-spender image, Las Vegas retaliates with an after-dinner drink called the High Limit Kir Royale for $2,200. If you've brought your girlfriend along, that's $4,400 for a single drink for each of you, and you still have to pay for dinner.

Nothing our ancestors would consider "drinking," which may be the whole point.

We have vodka to blame. Before it hit our shores, much of what you put in your drink had a flavor of its own. Who put chocolate syrup in their rum or produced a lemon-flavored Scotch? Vodka, previously associated with Russian and Polish peasants who couldn't afford European wines and brewed it in the cellar from leftover potatoes, arrived in America in the 1930s from Smirnoff ("It Leaves You Breathless"): when you came back to the office, nobody could smell what you'd had for lunch.

Plain, tasteless vodka became the drink of choice for people who didn't like drinking but wanted to get drunk. Another advantage was that, being tasteless, it lent itself to a vast array of ingredients. It began to take over; it put on sophisticated airs and muscled into the martini. It replaced soda water as the neutral substance ready for any insult that came to hand, from vanilla extract to chili powder, and bartender vied with bartender for the oddest flavorings.

By 1976 vodka had become the best-selling spirit in the country. Gin all but disappeared. It may be that the American passion for vodka has eighteenth-century roots: vodka isn't gin. While lowly rum, thanks to its seagoing history, still holds on to a certain yo-ho-ho swashbuckle, gin is tainted by an urban miasma: the steppes of Russia trump the slums of London. "Gin was mother's milk to her," said Eliza Doolittle. In the mid-nineteenth century a temperance ode declared:

Gin! Gin! A glass of gin!
What magnified monsters encircle therein!
Ragged and stained with filth and mud,
Some plague-spotted, and some with blood,
Shapes of misery, shame and sin!
Figures that make us loathe and tremble,
Creatures scarce human, that more resemble
Broods of diabolical kin,
Ghoul and vampire, Demon and din.
Gin! Gin! A Glass of Gin!
THE DRAM OF SATAN! THE LIQUOR OF SIN!

Hardly a drink to order in an air-conditioned bar with leather banquettes. Vodka came to us unstained by filth, mud, and blood, innocent of any history we'd heard, and it can't be denounced in verse since nothing rhymes with it.

As the twentieth century wound down, vodka branched out in new and different flavors, bland and sweet; peach and lime. Never vulgar, never smelling of itself the way whiskey does. It inspired the sophisticated to more fanciful flights; a new technique among the chic calls for inhaling it. This is hard on the nasal passages, and the thought of breathing rather than swallowing our cocktail seems counterintuitive, but apparently the method delivers a convivial kick, though it must look odd in a restaurant.

According to their ads, a Canadian vodka distillery sends a man out into the waters off the coast of Newfoundland to shoot a powerful cannon at icebergs, breaking them into manageable chunks, fishing them out and hauling them home to melt and make into vodka. These waters, the distillery's president brags, are "the purest in the world," having been sealed into ice thousands of years ago and therefore free of modern pollutants.

A long way from the Russian peasant distilling his left-over potatoes into what he called "dear little water."

Some of the old standbys survive. Even whiskey is still to be had, though you wouldn't want to drink it just plain. A concoction enjoying current success with the young is called the Three Wise Men and consists of Jim Beam bourbon, Johnnie Walker Scotch, and Jack Daniel's Tennessee sour mash. The combination has been implicated in the deaths of several young people celebrating their twenty-first birthdays, but danger just adds to the glamour.

After all, the whole point of fermented and distilled beverages is that you feel better while drinking them. Feeling better includes feeling more chic, more knowledgeable, and more sophisticated than the next man. Or, in some cases, braver.

As of this writing, though, neither fitness nor the thousand-dollar raspberry cocktail has penetrated deep into the American heartland.

Some people in Kansas and Montana and Arkansas still go into a bar and say, "Hey, Pete. What's happening? Give me a beer." And turn to the man on the next stool and say, "How's your mom?"

Appendix A—*Making Your Own*

Applejack

This was apparently a purely American breakthrough. Applejack is distilled by cold, not heat. Heat is easy to make compared with cold. No one has recorded who stumbled on the idea, but newcomers to these shores from the British Isles must have been astonished at the winter temperatures in New England. Undaunted, they turned them to good use.

Start with apple wine; at 10 or 12 percent alcohol, it's already a bit more powerful than 5 percent hard cider, a natural product arrived at by simple neglect (see below). Depending on how awful the winter is, applejack can come in as powerful as whiskey while still tasting of apples. Store your finished apple wine at below-freezing temperatures. The water in the wine freezes and rises to the top, while the alcohol stands pat. Every day you scoop off the ice that burgeons up, leaving the alcohol and the appleness behind to get more and more concentrated.

Every day there will be less and less ice, until no more will freeze at that temperature. At zero degrees, you'll have 14 percent alcohol; at ten below it gets up to 20 percent; at thirty below you can get 33 percent, or 66 proof, a great comfort in winter in Vermont. By the first thaw it's ready to drink, and by then you need a drink.

Modern advisers tell us we can get the same effect in our home freezer, but mine doesn't get down to thirty below. They also suggest we could get the same effect using pears, watermelons, peaches, or strawberries, but few people grow watermelons where the winters get to thirty below.

Apple Wine

Take sweet cider from the very best apples immediately from the press. Strain it through a flannel bag into a tub, and stir into it as much honey as will make it strong enough to bear up an egg. (Eggs figure prominently in drinks recipes.) Then boil it and skim it, and when the scum ceases to rise, strain it again. When cool, put it into a cask, and set it in a cool cellar till spring. Then bottle it off, and when ripe it will be found a very pleasant beverage. (Or you can go on to the applejack phase.)

Elderberry Wine

In Frank Capra's 1944 classic movie, *Arsenic and Old Lace*, the hero's sweet maiden aunts are uncovered as having poisoned various lonely old men with their homemade elderberry wine, convinced they were doing them a favor.

4 lbs elderberries
1 gallon boiling water

3 lbs sugar
1 packet activated yeast
8 ozs chopped raisins
juice of 1 lemon and 1 lime
1 tsp of yeast nutrient

Strip berries with a fork into a large fermentation kettle. Add raisins, lemon and orange juice, yeast nutrient. Add boiling water, stir. When cool, squeeze berries with hands to extract juice. Let sit one day. Add 2½ pounds of sugar and activated yeast. Leave covered three days. Strain liquid into demijohns, add a quarter pound sugar to each, and leave to ferment in a cool dark place. When bubbling subsides, strain into a clean demijohn. Six weeks later, strain again. When clear and quiet, bottle and age at least six months.

The aunts added to the recipe:

1 tsp arsenic
½ tsp strychnine
a pinch of cyanide

Dandelion Wine

1 quart dandelion blossoms, packed down
1 gallon water
1 lemon, sliced
2½ lbs sugar
2 tbsps good yeast

Put all in a kettle except yeast. Boil five minutes. Pour into jar. When cold, add yeast. Keep in a warm place three days until it ferments, then strain, bottle, and cork tightly.

Blackberry Wine

Measure your berries and bruise them. To every gallon add one quart of boiling water. Let the mixture stand twenty-four hours, stirring occasionally, then strain off the liquor into a cask. To every gallon add two pounds of sugar; cork tightly, and let stand till the following October.

Peach Brandy

Peel peaches but do not stone. Put half an inch of sugar into a wide-mouth half-gallon jar, then add a layer of peaches. Cover peaches with sugar, carefully filling in spaces. Repeat layers of sugar and peaches, finishing with sugar. Seal, then let stand six months to ripen. Drain and bottle liquid. Peaches may be eaten as dessert.

Frozen Potato Wine

When an early frost freezes your potato crop, as long as they're not soft and waterish, crush or bruise them with a mallet or put them through the cider press. To one bushel, add ten gallons of water boiled with a half pound of hops and a quarter pound of ginger. Pour the water over the potatoes and let it stand for three days, and then add yeast. When the fermentation has subsided, draw off the liquor into a cask and add half a pound of sugar for every gallon. After three months it will be ready to drink.

Appendix B—*Starting Your Still*

Start with rye, brown sugar, cracked corn, and raisins. You need fifty-gallon wooden barrels, preferably made of white oak, charred inside and held together with metal hoops.

The rye was coated with wax to prevent weevils and such from spoiling it, so to remove the wax you put fifty pounds of rye in a gunnysack and soak it in a washtub until it swells up and the wax falls off. Then drain off the waxy water and put the soaked rye in a fifty-gallon barrel with fifty pounds of sugar, twenty-five gallons of water, and around three gallons of the warm beer, which had the yeast in it to start the fermentation and got dipped out of your previous batch that was being cooked off.

Mix it all together and cover the barrel with a gunnysack to keep out leaves and debris.

Modern folks have a hydrometer to regulate the sugar content. It measures the specific gravity of the stuff; it reads "10" when you've got the right mix, and then "0" when your mixture is completely fermented and ready to be cooked off in the still.

If you don't have a hydrometer, use half a raw potato.

Drop it in, and if it floats, the sugar content is too high; add water until it starts to sink, but not clear to the bottom. It should kind of hover.

Use the one batch of rye up to six times, then add around twenty pounds of cracked corn and use it as much as twice more. If you can afford them, add ground raisins, which can get you up to a sixth run and produce "whiskey supreme."

In cold weather, put some warm bricks in the barrels to help move things along. When the bubbles stop rising to the surface, the yeast has converted all the sugar into alcohol and the brew is ready to be cooked off. Strain it through a sack to get out the rye and whatever else is in there, and pour it into the cooker. Heat it to boil off the alcohol.

Make the heater from a fifty-gallon drum cut down to size and installed on metal bed rails, cut so the heater can slide in and out under the cooker to regulate the heat, so it doesn't get too hot, boil over into the condensation coils, and go sour and nasty. Keep ready a "puke pot" attached to the cooker to trap overflow and send it back into the whiskey.

Connect a two-inch brass "T" to the top of the cooler (see illustration). A brass plug screwed into the two-inch pipe can be taken out when the beer is poured into the cooker and then put back. Attach a copper pipe at a right angle to the T, and fasten this to the copper condenser coil, which fits into a wooden barrel filled with cold water. At its far end, the coil sticks out of the barrel; plug it with cotton to keep water from leaking. Add more cool water as necessary to keep the proper temperature.

As the brew is heated in the cooker, the alcohol boils

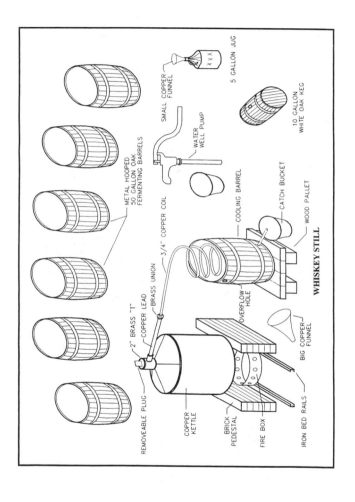

WHISKEY STILL

off at a lower temperature than water, and its vapor rises and gets forced into the coil, then reverts to liquid alcohol to be poured off into whatever jugs, kegs, or crocks you have handy. It's very basic stuff, and the artistic will want to enhance it.

To test the proof of your product, put some in a jar and shake it up. Then check the bubbles. At 100 proof, you will see about nine glistening bubbles and they won't burst. At 180 proof, the bubbles will be fewer and bigger and burst almost at once.

To add a whiskey-like color to the spirits, a purist uses toasted white-oak chips, but it's easier to pour in a little brown-sugar syrup. To sell it as gin instead, a few drops of juniper oil will give it the distinctive flavor, but it's easier to boil up the tender shoots of pine seedlings until you have a woodsy-smelling soup to pour in. Creative moonshiners will develop their own distinctive recipes based on the tastes of their clientele.

Selected Bibliography

Barr, Andrew. *Drink: A Social History*. London: Pimlico (Random House UK), 1995.

Blythe, Ronald. *Akenfield: Portrait of an English Village*. New York: Pantheon Books, 1969.

Brown, John Hull. *Early American Beverages*. Rutland, VT: Charles E. Tuttle, 1966.

Brown, Pete. *Man Walks into a Pub: A Sociable History of Beer*. London: Macmillan, 2003.

Burns, Eric. *Spirits of America: A Social History of Alcohol*. Philadelphia: Temple University Press, 2004.

Dickens, Cedric. *Drinking with Dickens*. New York: New Amsterdam Books, 1980.

Earle, Alice M. *Colonial Days in Old New York*. New York: C. Scribner's, Sons, 1896.

Frazer, James George. *The Golden Bough*. New York: Macmillan, 1940.

Hardwick, Michael, and Mollie Greenhalgh. *The Jolly Toper*. London: Herbert Jenkins, Ltd., 1961.

Lanza, Joseph. *The Cocktail: The Influence of Spirits on the American Psyche*. New York: St Martin's Press, 1995.

Lender, Mark Edward, and James Kirby Martin. *Drinking in America*, rev. ed. New York: Free Press, 1987.

Lendler, Ian. *Alcoholica Esoterica: A Collection of Useful and Useless Information as It Relates to the History and Consumption of All Manner of Booze*. New York: Penguin, 2005.

London, Jack. *John Barleycorn*. 1913; New York: Modern Library, 2001.

McCormick, Robert. *Facing Alcoholism*. San Diego, CA: Oak Tree, 1982.

Mississippi Department of Marine Resources. *Marine Resources and History of the Mississippi Gulf Coast*. Jackson: Mississippi Department of Marine Resources, 1998.

Moorehead, Alan. *The White Nile*, rev. ed. New York: Harper and Row, 1971.

Polo, Marco. *The Travels of Marco Polo, the Venetian*. Trans. and ed. William Marsden. Garden City, NY: Doubleday, 1948.

Rae, Simon, ed. *The Faber Book of Drink, Drinkers, and Drinking*. London: Faber, 1991.

Rorabaugh, William J. *The Alcoholic Republic: An American Tradition*. New York: Oxford University Press, 1979.

Schivelbusch, Wolfgang. *Tastes of Paradise: A Social History of Spices, Stimulants, and Intoxicants*. Trans. David Jacobson. New York: Pantheon Books, 1992.

Shakespeare, William. *Henry IV, Part II*. Act IV, Scene 2.

Willison, George F. *Saints and Strangers*. New York: Reynal and Hitchcock, 1945.

Woodforde, James. *The Diary of a Country Parson, 1758–1802*. Norwich, UK: Fletcher and Son, 1969.

A Note on the Author

Barbara Holland is the author of fifteen previous books, including *Hail to the Chiefs, They Went Whistling, Gentlemen's Blood,* and, most recently, *When All the World Was Young*. She lives in Virginia's Blue Ridge Mountains.